No Ro…
For Lo…

A Farce

ANTHONY MARRIOTT
and
BOB GRANT

SAMUEL FRENCH

LONDON
NEW YORK TORONTO SYDNEY HOLLYWOOD

ISBN 0 573 11310 6

NO ROOM FOR LOVE

First performed at the Theatre Royal, Brighton, on the 19th May 1975, with the following cast of characters:

The Manager	Desmond Walter Ellis
Albert	Hugh Paddick
Dr Garfield	Kenneth Connor
Michele	Hilary Pritchard
Mrs Garfield	Thora Hird
Julie	Gay Soper
Clifford	Barry Evans
Douglas	John Blythe
Evelyn	Sheila Staefel

The play directed by Edgar Metcalfe
Setting by J. Hutchinson Scott

The action takes place during one summer night at the Lawns Hotel, Kingstanton, Suffolk

ACT I Evening
ACT II Later

Time—the present

Please note our NEW ADDRESS:

Samuel French Ltd
52 Fitzroy Street London W1P 6JR
Tel: 01 - 387 9373

ACT I

The interior of the first floor of The Lawns Hotel, Kingstanton. Evening

The hotel has seen better days, though not much better, but it still retains a seedy charm from an earlier period. To one side is a corridor, from which there is the entrance to a lift, and above it the door to Room 18. The corridor continues off upstage, with doors to Room 12 and Room 11 respectively: the latter is just off stage. Occupying most of the stage is Room 12a (*alias 13*), *the bridal suite, with a door leading into the corridor. In Room 12 there is a double bed, beside it a bed table on which there is a carafe of water and a glass. Above it is a wall-mounted dial telephone. In the corner below it is a small armchair, and beside this a wastepaper-basket. In the rear wall french windows lead off to a communal balcony. Opposite the bed is a door to the bathroom which has been created by partitioning off a corner of the room. Below it a door leads to a minute dressing-room; above this is a mirror on the wall. Across the front of the stage a strip of moth-eaten carpet indicates the continuation of the corridor, at the far end of which is the door to Room 14. The corridor runs off past this room. There is no number on the door of the bridal suite. All the locks on the door are mortise locks. There are linked light switches above the bed and by the main door, and a hanging bowl-lamp above the bed. A notice at the upstage end of the corridor reads "Stairs and Fire Exit", and a similar notice pointing off the downstage end, reading "To Bathroom and W.C".*

As the CURTAIN *rises to the accompaniment of instruments tuning up in various parts of the hotel, the Manager enters from the upstage corridor, talking off towards Room 11. He is a fussy, self-important man, in black jacket and pin-striped trousers*

Manager Yes, sir, your drinks are on the way. A large brandy and a small white wine wasn't it?

Man's Voice (*off*) No, you fool. A pint of bitter and a Babycham.

The lift indicator moves from "G" to "1"

Manager Oh yes, of course, sir, the others were for number thirty-four, the cor anglais and the tubular bells. You're the cello and the piccolo aren't you?

A loud vulgar bass note comes from the double bassoon, off. The Manager winces

Oh, these terrible musicians. (*He takes out a pocket perfume spray and sprays himself*) Ah, thank goodness. The drinks at last.

The lift arrives. We hear the expanding metal gate of the lift clang open, then the two solid wooden doors swing open. Albert, the only porter, comes out. He is belligerent and thoroughly miserable. He is allergic to work in any form. He carries a small tray on which are a pint of bitter and a Babycham

Albert Here's your drinks for Number Eleven. They're all spilt, the lift's gone wobbly again.
Manager You can't serve them like that, Albert. This is a first-class hotel.
Albert What, has it changed hands while I was downstairs?
Manager Certainly not!
Albert (*sniffing*) Cor, what a pong of perfume.
Manager (*sniffing*) I can't smell anything.
Albert No, you wouldn't.
Manager Now, do something about those drinks.
Albert Right. Cop hold of them.

The Manager takes the glasses off the tray. Albert pours the spillings from the tray into the two glasses

Manager You can't do that, Albert.
Albert I've just done it. Don't matter, those stupid musicians won't know the difference. Babycham for the bloke with the piccolo and a pint of bitter for the lady cellist. (*He gets a cello in a case out of the lift*)
Manager Surely it must be the other way round.
Albert Well, you've seen the lady cellist, what do you reckon!
Manager Well, yes, you may be right.
Albert 'Ere, does she play this thing side-saddle or astride?
Manager Don't be so crude. The lady has one of the most beautiful instruments known to man.
Albert Yeah, and all she does is scratch it!
Manager There's no need to be vulgar. Give me those—(*he takes the tray of drinks*)—and get their luggage out of the lift at once.

Albert takes a piccolo case out of the lift and hands it to the Manager

Albert 'Eere y'are. Grab 'old of that.
Manager It's no good giving it to me. What am I supposed to do with it?
Albert (*muttering inaudibly*) Stuff it up your flue!
Manager What did you say?
Albert I've got enough to do. I must get hold of the old girl's fiddle and that's a two-handed job. And their luggage as well.

The Manager goes to Room 11

Albert gets the cases and the cello (in its case) out of the lift and closes the doors

Flamin' musicians. It's the same every year. I don't mind them having a music festival, but I wish they'd leave their instruments at home.

The Manager returns with the empty tray. He takes out a bottle of after-shave and dabs some on his face. Albert reacts

Manager By the way, Albert, I've had a message: Miss Burridge, the lady harpist, has been taken ill in the buffet at St Pancras Station.
Albert That makes a change. They're usually taken ill in our dining-room.
Manager Nonsense. So she won't be occupying Room Eighteen.
Albert Good. That's all I need to bring on my allergies, a dirty great harp.
Manager But they're sending a deputy, a Mrs Garfield.
Albert They would. Well, she can carry her own blasted 'arp.
Manager That's enough, Albert. I hope the bridal suite's ready for Mr and Mrs Smith.
Albert Cor blimey. What do they play? The Wurlitzer?
Manager No, no, they're not musicians, they're on their honeymoon. They're not going to play anything.
Albert Huh, funny sort of honeymoon. Anyway, we haven't got a bridal suite.
Manager Of course we have, Twelve A.
Albert You mean Thirteen.
Manager You mustn't call it Thirteen. Some people are very superstitious. One does want honeymooners to get off to a good start.
Albert They're not gonna start at all if they don't play anything. Anyway, what have they got two rooms for?
Manager What are you talking about, Albert?
Albert I saw it on the sheet. Room Twelve Mr and Mrs Smith, Room Twelve A Mr and Mrs Smith. What's the matter with 'em, are they separated already? (*He laughs*)
Manager No, no, Albert, that stupid receptionist girl's made a mistake. She's always doing it, she put them down twice. Albert, I told you yesterday to put the new number on the door.
Albert I couldn't the chef pinched me screwdriver to prick the sausages with.

Albert goes into Room 11 with the luggage

Manager Oh, really. (*He goes into 12a*)

The lift starts to go down. The Manager looks round 12a, straightens the curtains, goes into the bathroom, comes out with an aerosol spray and sprays the pillows, then himself. Noises of instruments are heard, off

If music be the food of love, they won't go hungry tonight. (*He goes into the corridor*)

Albert enters

Albert Thank you for nothing.
Manager How many times must I tell you, Albert. You mustn't solicit for gratuities.
Albert I wasn't, I was asking for a tip.
Manager Service is inclusive, I keep telling you.
Albert Yes, sir. (*He picks up a bag of tools which is on the floor by the bed*)
Manager What are those doing in here?
Albert The sash window in the bathroom wanted fixing. It wouldn't open.

Manager Have you fixed it?
Albert Oh, I've fixed it all right. It won't close now.
Manager Oh! Can't you do anything right? You'll have to do something about one of the beds in Fourteen. It's got a wobbly leg.
Albert What again? Must have been that Darby and Joan Club. Same every year. At their age they ought to know beds is for sleeping in.
Manager Well, do it right away, the new guests could be here any minute.

Albert goes out of Room 12a towards Room 14. The Manager follows

And another thing, the wash-hand basin in Mrs Garfield's room's coming away from the wall again. It wants seeing to at once.
Albert Which comes first, at once or right away?
Manager Both.
Albert I can't be in two places at the same time.

The lift starts to come up

Tell you what, I'll have a bash at the leg—(*taking out a large hammer*)—and you have a go at Mrs Garfield's basin.
Manager What am I supposed to do with it?
Albert Screw it up. And if I know you, that's just what you will do. (*He chuckles*) It's only a couple of little nuts want tightening. (*He gives him a large wrench*) 'Ere y'are, this'll do it.

Albert exits into Room 14

Manager (*looking at the wrench*) Well, really. (*He gets out a cologne stick and rubs it on his forehead, then gets out a footspray and squirts it down his socks. He goes towards the lift as it arrives*)
Michele (*in the lift*) No, George, not in here. Wait till we get to our room.
Garfield (*in the lift*) I'm just trying a different grip.

The Manager reacts. The lift doors open and Dr Garfield putts a golf ball out of the lift, which hits the Manager's feet. He hops about and drops the wrench on his other foot

Dr Garfield comes out, holding a putter. He is a good-looking man trying to keep middle-age at bay with great energy

Mind out, you fool! You ruined a perfectly good putt.

Michele comes out of the lift with luggage. She is a delectable dish from every point of view

Manager Yes, sir. Good evening, sir. I'm the Manager. Can I be of assistance?

Garfield picks up the golf ball, and reacts

Garfield What an overpowering scent on this landing.
Manager Really sir? I hadn't noticed it.
Michele We're looking for our room.
Manager Oh yes, madam, what name?
Michele Miss Unsworth.

Garfield (*quickly*) Mrs Smith. Mr and Mrs Smith. Er—she hasn't had time to get used to her married name yet, have you, my dear.

Manager Ah yes, Mr Smith, of course. You and your good lady are having the bridal suite, naturally, being on your honeymoon. Allow me, madam. (*He gets luggage from Michele*)

Michele Honeymoon? We're not on our honeymoon.

Garfield shoots her an anxious look

Manager But I thought . . .

Garfield Ah, what Miss—er—Mrs Smith meant was we're not on honeymoon as far as anyone else is concerned. We don't want any embarrassment, do we, my dear?

Manager (*leading the way to Room 12a*) One quite understands, sir. One will be the soul of discretion. This is your balcony, sir, lovely view of the North Sea—on a clear day. (*He opens the windows*) You have a nice dressing-room. I'll put your cases in there. (*He does so*)

Garfield Call that a dressing-room? It's no bigger than a cupboard.

Manager It was before we converted it. That's your bathroom through there. Anything else I can do for you, sir?

Garfield (*looking at Michele*) No, thank you.

Michele But I'm hungry. I want something to eat.

Garfield But we had dinner on the way here.

Michele That was nearly an hour ago. I'm hungry again now.

Manager That'll be our bracing sea air. Would madam like a little something up in her room?

Garfield Yes, that's what we're here for.

Manager Would madam like some food?

Michele Yes, that'll be lovely.

Manager I'm afraid at this time of night you can only have sandwiches. You'll be wanting champagne, naturally.

Michele That'll be lovely.

Manager I'll send the porter up with your order directly. Good-night, madam, sir. I hope you don't mind my mentioning it, please don't tip the porter—our service is inclusive.

The Manager goes into the corridor, shutting the door behind him, picks up the wrench and goes into Room 18

Garfield Michele, you must be more careful. You nearly gave the game away, calling yourself Miss Unsworth.

Michele It's so old fashioned, George, all this pretending to be Mr and Mrs Smith. You didn't have to tell the Manager we were on our honeymoon.

Garfield Well, it is our first time together. A sort of trial honeymoon.

Michele Well, that's all right so long as you do marry me.

Garfield Of course I will, eventually. There's just one small problem.

Michele What's that?

Garfield My wife. She can be very vindictive. You see I put the house and everything in her name for tax purposes.

Michele That was a silly thing to do.

Garfield Not entirely. It was her money in the first place.

Michele The trouble with your wife is that she doesn't understand you like I do. Anyway that's no problem, it's so easy to get a divorce these days. And I do so want to be the second Mrs Garfield. I want everyone to know about us. I feel like shouting it from the rooftops.

Garfield No, no, don't do that. You don't seem to realize what a risk I'm running, taking you away for the week-end. I could be struck off.

Michele Don't be ridiculous—you can't be struck off just for spending the week-end in a hotel with your receptionist, even if you are married.

Garfield You're not just my receptionist, you're my patient as well. That's why I picked this hotel, no chance of meeting any of my friends.

Michele Well I was looking forward to a nice week-end in a decent hotel in Brighton, with a bit of dancing.

Garfield We couldn't go to Brighton. My wife's spending the week-end there with her sister. She's the only one who appreciates my wife's harp playing—she's stone deaf.

Michele Well why did we have to come to this terrible place in the middle of nowhere?

Garfield That's the whole idea. I don't know anyone in Kingstanton. (*He picks up the golf bag and puts it in the dressing-room*) Shan't be needing these.

Michele What did you bring them for then?

Garfield I had to. I told Winifred I was playing golf in Cromer.

The telephone rings

Michele (*picking up the receiver*) Dr Garfield's surgery. Miss Unsworth speaking.

Garfield reacts

Er—I mean Mrs Smith. . . . Oh that'll be lovely, thank you. Yes, we would like a magnum. (*She puts down the receiver*) That was the Manager, he's sending up a magnum, isn't that nice of him.

Garfield I'm not all that keen on champagne. I could do with a Scotch.

Michele Well let's go down to the bar and have a drink. (*She picks up her make-up case*)

Garfield Yes all right, come on. (*He takes her left hand in his right, opens the door, reacts and looks at her hand*) Oh my God, you haven't got a wedding ring on!

Michele Well of course I haven't. I'm not married yet.

Garfield (*quickly shutting the door*) Ssh! Somebody might hear you. Put your gloves on.

Michele I haven't got any with me.

Garfield Well here you are, put my driving gloves on. (*He takes a pair of string-backed gloves from his pocket*)

Michele Don't be silly, George. I can't sit at the bar drinking gin and tonic in those. I'll look ridiculous.

Garfield I know, you can wear my signet ring. (*He takes it off his little finger and gives it to her*)
Michele But it's got the initials G.G. on it.
Garfield Yes G.G. I know you can say it's your great grandmother's. G.G.

They laugh

Come on.

They go towards the lift; it starts to go down

Blast, missed it. We'll go down the stairs.

Michele and Garfield go off upstage. Albert comes out of Room 14 carrying his bag of tools

Albert Soon done that.

There is a crash of breaking a wash-basin in Room 18 and a cry from the Manager

Sounds like he's done it and all.

The Manager limps on from Room 18, holding a piece of the wash-basin

Manager Albert, I've had an accident in the basin.
Albert Screwed it up, 'ave you? I said you would. (*He drops the bag on the floor*)
Manager You gave me the wrong implement. Have you fixed the bed-leg in Fourteen?

The lift starts to come up

Albert Yes.
Manager Thank goodness for that. And it isn't loose any more?
Albert No it isn't, it's come off completely. (*He takes a bed-leg out of his bag*)
Manager What? You can't have a bed with only three legs.
Albert I know you can't. That's why I took them off an' all. (*He takes out the other three bed-legs*)
Manager You're ruining this hotel.
Albert You can't ruin a ruin.
Manager Go downstairs at once.

The lift doors open

And take that awful old bag with you.

Mrs Garfield comes out of the lift. She is a handsome, forceful lady

Mrs Garfield I beg your pardon? How dare you.
Manager Oh I'm terribly sorry, madam, I didn't see you there.
Mrs Garfield And who might you be?
Manager I'm the Manager, madam.
Mrs Garfield Well you're not managing very well. I've had to carry my own harp.

Manager Harp? Oh are you Mrs Garfield?

Mrs Garfield Of course I am. What an extraordinary scent there is on this landing.

Manager I can't smell anything, but I'm trying to remove it.

Albert You wanna remove yourself.

Manager Albert, attend to the lady's luggage at once.

Albert gives him a dirty look and goes into the lift

Mrs Garfield Be careful with that harp. It's a very delicate and valuable instrument! (*She turns to the manager*) It's all been a terrible rush. I was with my sister in Brighton, you know, when they phoned. And now here I am playing in the opening concert of the Festival tomorrow. I wasn't even able to let my husband know. (*She takes her own pulse*) Oh dear, my pulse rate's right up. I knew it would be. I'd better do some of my Yoga breathing. (*She takes some deep breaths*)

Manager I hope madam isn't unwell.

Mrs Garfield I am now. It's that terrible scent.

Manager Perhaps I should call a doctor.

Mrs Garfield No need for that. My husband's a doctor so I've had to cure myself for years. (*She feels her pulse again*) It's right down now. I might have to stop breathing altogether.

Manager Oh dear, please don't distress yourself madam. Would you like me to contact your husband?

Mrs Garfield You can't do that. He's not at home. He's playing golf somewhere round Cromer.

Albert drags a harp out of the lift

Don't drag it, man, lift it. You'll scrape my pedal box.

Albert What's it got pedals for, it's not a bicycle.

Mrs Garfield (*to the Manager*) I tried to contact my husband's receptionist —for his number, but she wasn't there. I suppose she's taken the week-end off just because he's away. The trouble with that girl is she doesn't understand him like I do. When I married him and set him up in practice, *I* was his first receptionist, you know. I started him playing golf as well.

Manager Oh really, madam, do you play yourself?

Mrs Garfield Oh I love it, when I can get a game, but of course my music comes first.

Albert drops the harp

For heaven's sake, man, have you no respect for music?

Albert Music? I'm the hotel porter, not the Archangel Gabriel. (*He picks up the harp and takes it into Room 18*)

Manager If you like golf, madam, I've noticed one of our other guests has brought his clubs. Should you care to play while you're here, perhaps I could arrange a game with him.

Mrs Garfield Oh, that would be nice. I wonder what his handicap is?

Manager I don't know, madam. He's here on his honeymoon.

Mrs Garfield Oh well, that might be a bit of a handicap. I mean if he's here with his new wife, I can't expect him to play with me.

Manager No, of course not, madam.

Mrs Garfield Never mind, with a bit of luck I might be able to meet up with my husband. Cromer's quite near here isn't it?

Manager Yes, madam. About twenty miles, as the crow flies.

Albert comes back to pick up the rest of the luggage, and takes it into Room 18

Albert She'll be able to fly there then, won't she.

Manager Albert! Will you excuse me, madam. I'm expecting the brass section any moment.

Mrs Garfield Well don't put them next door to me. They sit up all night swilling beer, singing songs and playing strip poker with the chamber maids.

Albert returns from Room 18

Albert We've only got one and she's not what you'd call a full house.

Manager Don't worry, madam, I always put the brass section in the annexe, so that the porter can look after them.

The Manager goes off upstage

Albert Well, I'm not playing strip poker with 'em.

Mrs Garfield Right, that will be all, Porter. I don't wish to be disturbed. I wish to practice my Sibelius.

Mrs Garfield goes into Room 18

Albert Blimey, you're not going to play that harp up here are you. You'll frighten the life out of the other guests, they'll think they've passed over.

Mrs Garfield reappears from Room 18

Mrs Garfield What a frightful little room. And there's a hole in the basin.

Albert That was the Manager. He broke it when he was mending it.

Mrs Garfield Disgraceful! Every time I wash my hands I'm going to get wet feet.

Albert Bathroom's down that way, madam. (*He indicates the downstage exit*)

Mrs Garfield I wouldn't have stayed in this hotel if I could have got in anywhere else.

Albert No, they're all full up. It's your perishin' Music Festival in' it? All them bloomin' musicians, scraping, blowing and banging all day and all night. Brings on me allergies every year.

Mrs Garfield I shall require a call at eight o'clock with tea and *The Times*, and a glass of hot malted milk before retiring.

Albert (*muttering under his breath*) Bollocks.

Mrs Garfield (*sharply*) What did you say?

Albert Horlicks! I'll bring it up to you.

Mrs Garfield What a dreadful hotel.

Albert Yes it is. You wouldn't catch me stopping here. Service is awful.

The A.A. should have struck us off years ago. Right, I'll be going, madam. (*He holds out his hand*)

Mrs Garfield Very well, that'll be all.

Albert All? Haven't you forgotten something?

Mrs Garfield No. I've got all my luggage in spite of your efforts to the contrary.

The lift starts to go down

Albert It is usual to offer a gratuity for me trouble.

Mrs Garfield Service is inclusive.

Albert Not 'umping 'eavy 'arps isn't.

Mrs Garfield Oh very well. (*She opens her bag and takes out a tenpenny piece*) Have you got change of ten p.?

Albert No.

Mrs Garfield Pity. (*She puts the coin back in her bag*)

Mrs Garfield goes into Room 18 and closes the door

The lift starts to come up

Albert Right. That's cold Horlicks and yesterday's *Times*.

He sees the lift indicator start to move from "G" to "1"

Better make myself scarce—that might be the pianist.

Albert goes off upstage. The lift arrives. Michelle comes out followed by Dr Garfield

Michele (*a little giggly*) It was nice of you to buy me that half-bottle of champagne. I'm feeling all bubbly inside.

Garfield (*happily*) Yes, just what the doctor ordered.

Michele Yes, I think I'm ready for anything now.

Garfield And you've still got a whole magnum to go.

They go into Room 12a

Michele Oh, what have I done with my make-up case?

Garfield (*indulgently*) Silly girl. You must have left it in the bar. Shall I fetch it for you?

Michele Oh you are a dear. You don't mind if I don't come with you, I don't think I could make the trip. To tell you the truth, I'm feeling a teeny, weeny bit squiffy.

The lift goes down

Garfield Don't you worry, my dear. You pop out on the balcony and get a bit of sea air. We don't want you passing out, do we. (*He chuckles*)

Michele No, that wouldn't be much fun, would it.

Garfield Shan't be a minute. (*He opens the door*)

Michele Oh, darling Dr Garfield, I do so love you.

Garfield Ssh! (*He shuts the door quickly*)

As he does so, Mrs Garfield pokes her head out of Room 18

The lift comes up

Mrs Garfield Did somebody call? (*She sees there is no-one in the corridor*)

Mrs Garfield goes back to her room

Michele (*mouthing*) Love you.
Garfield (*mouthing*) Fancy you, too.

Michele goes on to the balcony, and off the opposite side to the upstage corridor

Garfield goes out of Room 12a and to the lift

Think I'll have a quick double while I'm down there. Must last the course.

The sound of a harp comes from Room 18

Wish my wife could play like that.

The lift doors open and Albert comes out carrying a new suitcase. He is followed by Clifford and Julie Smith. Clifford is a diffident and naïve young man. He is dressed in a new off-the-peg suit. Julie, his bride of a few hours, is younger, and is pretty in a doll-like way but very nervous. She is over-dressed in her going-away clothes

Albert This way, Mr and Mrs Smith.

Garfield enters the lift and goes down

Julie Oh, it is a nice hotel, Clifford.
Clifford I'm glad you like it, Julie. Mr Johnson of Kitchenware highly recommended it. His cousin came here for the Music Festival once.
Albert This is your room, Twelve A. What they call the bridal suite. Have you got the key, sir?
Clifford No, I thought you had it.
Albert Makes no difference. The lock's broken anyway.
Julie Oh dear. Clifford, you'll have to put a chair against the door. Somebody might come into us.

Music is heard off

Albert (*shouting*) Shut up! Don't worry, they'll all be too busy scraping and blowing and banging their instruments.

Clifford and Julie go into Room 12a and look around

Mrs Garfield comes out of Room 18

Mrs Garfield Porter, I'd like some biscuits with my malted milk.
Albert (*muttering under his breath*) Nackers!
Mrs Garfield What did you say?
Albert Crackers. We've only got cream crackers.
Mrs Garfield Oh, very well. I suppose they'll have to do.
Albert Yes, they will.

Mrs Garfield goes into Room 18 and shuts the door

Albert goes into Room 12a

Julie Oh, this is a lovely room, Clifford, like a dream come true.
Clifford I never thought this day would come, Julie. I must be the luckiest man in the world. Alone together, just the two of us. You and me.
Albert (*dropping the case behind them with a thud*) And me. There's your case.
Clifford Oh, thank you very much.
Albert That's your bathroom, useless plumbing. That's your dressing-room, pokey little hole. May I wish you every happiness, sir.
Clifford Oh, thank you.

Pause. Albert stands his ground

(*Whispering to Julie*) What's he waiting for?
Clifford Oh yes of course. (*He gives Albert a coin*) Thank you very much.
Albert May I wish Mrs Smith every happiness as well.
Clifford (*giving him another coin*) That's very kind of you.
Albert May I wish you both every happiness as well.
Clifford (*not giving any money*) Thank you.

Albert realizes he will get no more

Albert Yes. (*He goes to the door*) Good job service is inclusive.

Albert pockets the money and goes out along the upstage corridor

There is an awkward pause

Clifford Well, little Squirrel.
Julie Well, big Badger.

Another pause

Clifford Here we are, on our own at last.
Julie At last.
Clifford Just think, we've got a whole week-end alone together.
Julie All those lovely concerts. Just to think, we'd been working in the same store for two years and never met, and it took that concert last year to bring us together.
Clifford Yes, it was wonderful, the London Transport Symphony Orchestra.
Julie Do you remember when they played the "Surprise Symphony" and my hand found yours?
Clifford Yes that was a surprise.
Julie And now here we are on a musical honeymoon.
Clifford Yes. I thought the staff at the store gave us a jolly good send-off, didn't you?
Julie Yes, the canteen looked ever so festive. So nice of mother to lend us her Christmas decorations. She's quite right, it was much nicer than flowers.
Clifford Yes, I suppose it was nicer.

Julie Mother looked nice in her organza frock. She sewed on all those sequins herself you know.

Clifford Yes, very nice.

Julie The presents were nice, too. Lovely fondue set from your fellow salesmen in the Bedding Department.

Clifford Yes, we shall be able to have some Swiss evenings. I thought it was highly original of your colleagues in Baby-wear to give us those escargot dishes.

Julie Yes, we shall be able to have some French evenings as well. Mind you, I don't know whether I'm going to like snails. What do they taste like?

Clifford Well, I don't know exactly, but I'm sure they're delicious. I say, old Jenkins from Hardware got a bit tiddly didn't he?

Julie Yes he did. I was quite surprised, him being a chief buyer.

Clifford I thought one or two of his jokes went a bit far for mixed company.

Julie I didn't understand that one about the honeymoon couple who couldn't get to sleep because he wanted to get up early. I don't see the point of it. Was he a long-distance lorry driver?

Clifford (*embarrassed*) Well, I think he told it wrong. He was on his fourth cream sherry by then. (*He notices the bed for the first time*) My word, I do believe that is a Sleepwell RT Seventeen. (*He lifts the cover*) Yes it's even got the optional striped ticking.

Julie Fancy that. I must say you certainly know your trade.

Clifford So I should, I've been working in beds ever since I left saucepans.

Julie Yes, your career has gone well.

Clifford (*warming to his subject*) Mind you, we gave up stocking RT Seventeens. Had no end of complaints about them. People just didn't get the wear out of them. And the springs were far too tensile. They kept popping through.

Julie I hope it's safe.

Clifford Don't worry, they're safe enough, if you know how to use them. All we have to do, Squirrel, is to watch ourselves, be careful, nothing too violent.

Julie Oh, Clifford. (*She hiccups several times*)

Clifford Poor Squirrel, has she got nasty hiccups?

Julie I—(*hic*)—always do—(*hic*)—whenever—(*hic*)—anyone—(*hic*)—talks about—(*hic*)—"it".

Clifford What do you mean, Squirrel—"it"?

Julie It—(*hic*)—you know—(*hic*)—"it".

Clifford "It"?

Julie You know S—E—X. (*Hic, hic, hic*)

Clifford Why didn't you tell me before?

Julie I didn't—(*hic*)—like to—(*hic*)—I thought it might put you off me. (*Hic, hic*)

Clifford Well, I must say this is a bit of a shock. Isn't there anything that cures it?

Julie Oh yes, a glass of water. (*Hic*)

Clifford That's a relief.
Julie And change the subject.
Clifford Oh dear! (*He quickly pours a glass of water*) I think I'd better get them to send up some more carafes. Here you are, Squirrel. Soon be all better now.

He gives her a glass of water. She sips it, and stops hiccuping

Julie All gone now, Badger.
Clifford And they won't come back?
Julie No, they won't come back. As long as you don't mention "it" again.
Clifford But how are we going to—oh crumbs. Would you like to go down for a drink?
Julie Whatever for? I had a cream sherry at the reception.
Clifford Well, I thought it might help things.
Julie What things?
Clifford Well—you know—(*he gets a glass of water*)—"it"!

Julie hiccups, drinks water, she stops

Julie Don't let me stop you having a little drink. I don't want to spoil your fun.
Clifford (*miserably*) Oh I know that, Squirrel.
Julie Anyway, I want to wash my hands.
Clifford Oh, well I'll go down then, Squirrel. I'll just have a half of shandy.

Michelle appears in the french windows

Michele Sorry, I must have the wrong room. They all look alike from out here. I hope I didn't disturb you.
Clifford That's quite all right, we weren't doing anything.
Michele I must have passed it. Good-night.

Michele goes out to the balcony and off the corridor side

The lift starts to come up

Julie Off you go, Badger. Mind you just have half a pint. We don't want you getting up in the middle of the night. (*She hiccups*)
Clifford 'Bye, Squirrel. (*He waves to her*)
Julie 'Bye, Badger. (*She waves*) Come back to the burrow soon.
Clifford I will. (*He goes out to corridor*)

Julie goes into the bathroom, taking the case. The lift arrives, Garfield gets out, carrying a vanity case. Clifford goes into the lift and down

Garfield goes straight into Room 12a

Garfield Michele . . . Oh. (*He looks round, goes out to balcony, and calls*) Michele!

Garfield goes off the opposite side to Michele

Julie (*coming out of bathroom*) Is that you, Badger? (*She sees there is no-one there, goes back into the bathroom, and shuts the door*)

Michele enters upstage in corridor, moves down towards the door of Room 12a. At the same time Garfield comes in from the balcony into Room 12a

Garfield Where are you, Michele?

Julie comes out of bathroom

Julie Oh! A man! (*She hiccups*) Hic!
Garfield Oh, I'm terribly sorry, I must have the wrong room. All look the same.

Garfield goes off by the balcony to the corridor. Julie hiccups as she returns to the bathroom, closing the door

At the same moment Michele opens the bedroom door and enters Room 12a. She lifts her suitcase out of the dressing-room and starts to unpack it

Garfield enters the upstage corridor. As he reaches the door of Room 12a, Mrs Garfield comes out of Room 18, carrying a knitting-bag

Mrs Garfield Excuse me. Do you know where the T.V. lounge is?
Garfield (*half turning*) No, I'm afraid I don't. Oh my God! Winifred!
Mrs Garfield George!
Mrs Garfield
Garfield } What are *you* doing here? { *Speaking together*

Garfield gulps

Mrs Garfield Well?

Garfield "goldfishes"

What *are* you doing here?
Garfield Er—well—you see. What am I doing here. Ah! I'm doing here—what I'm doing here. What are *you* doing here?
Mrs Garfield I'm playing in the concert tomorrow.
Garfield Tomorrow? Then you're staying the night?
Mrs Garfield Well of course I am. I had an emergency call from the Festival. Amy Burridge has let them down again. I tried to get your number to phone you, but that wretched girl Michele had gone away.
Garfield Had she really? I wonder where she is?
Mrs Garfield That girl's never around when you want her. Well I must say, it's lovely to find you here. What on earth made you come to this dreadful dump? I thought you were supposed to be playing golf in Cromer.
Garfield Well, I am.
Mrs Garfield Well, you must have sliced your first shot very badly. You're twenty miles off the fairway.
Garfield You don't understand. I haven't started playing yet.
Mrs Garfield Well, I can see that. Even you couldn't hit a golf ball that far. So what are you doing here?

Garfield I'm not playing golf. I'm here to do something quite different. It's not pleasure, it's business. I had an emergency call, too.

Mrs Garfield From the theatre. Don't make me laugh. You can't play a note. When you play "Chopsticks" it sounds like a Chinese meal. They wouldn't want you at the theatre.

Garfield Ah! But that's just it, they do. The operating theatre, the local hospital.

Mrs Garfield But you're not a surgeon, you're only a G.P.

Garfield So I am. Ah, but it's one of my patients.

Mrs Garfield But your practice is in Bromley, you haven't got any patients in Kingstanton.

Garfield No, I haven't, have I. Not living in Kingstanton—just passing through. On holiday. That's it, I've got a patient in Kingstanton on holiday.

Mrs Garfield But why didn't he see a local doctor?

Garfield He did, and he sent for me because—er—he's very nervous about it.

Mrs Garfield What, the doctor?

Garfield No, my patient. He's very nervous because—they're operating on him in the morning.

Mrs Garfield Even so, fancy having the gall to interrupt your golf. What's he got?

Garfield Ah well, that's just what he's got hasn't he. He's got gallstones as big as golf balls.

Mrs Garfield Poor man. Is it anyone I know?

Garfield No, no, I hardly know him myself.

Mrs Garfield What's his name?

Garfield Er—Smith. Mr Smith.

Mrs Garfield Is that your room? (*She points to Room 12a*)

Garfield Er—yes—my patient booked it for me.

Mrs Garfield Well, I hope he's got you a decent one. You should see the pokey little hole they've put me in.

Garfield Really?

Mrs Garfield (*indicating Room 18*) See for yourself.

Garfield takes a quick look into Room 18

Garfield Not too bad.

In Room 12a Michele puts the case on the floor at the foot of the bed, carries a bundle of dresses into the dressing-room and shuts the door

At the same moment Mrs Garfield enters Room 12a

No! (*He follows her into Room 12a*)

Mrs Garfield What do you mean, no?

Garfield No good. This room's no good at all.

Mrs Garfield Nonsense. It's much nicer than mine. And it's a double, so I'll move in with you.

Garfield What!! I mean—what a good idea.

Mrs Garfield There's no point in squandering our money—my money. I'll move in right away.

Garfield No! I mean don't do that. (*Trying to usher her out*) Wouldn't you like a game of golf?

Mrs Garfield At this time of night? What are we going to use, luminous balls?

Garfield What a good idea.

Mrs Garfield Don't talk daft, George, it's too late to play now.

Garfield Yes, it's beginning to look like it.

Mrs Garfield (*taking a skein of wool out of her knitting-bag*) While you're here, you can make yourself useful. Hold your hands out.

He does so, holding the case over his arm, and she puts the wool on his hands

Garfield Let's go outside and do it. (*He goes to the door*)

Mrs Garfield What on earth for?

Garfield Er—there's more room in the corridor.

Mrs Garfield There's plenty of room in here. (*She finds the end and starts to wind wool*)

Garfield This looks remarkably like my golfing jumper.

Mrs Garfield It was. I never did like it. Now it's going to be a pair of bedsocks for the Church jumble. (*She stops winding*) Just a minute, what's that case?

Garfield What? Oh this. It's a case.

Mrs Garfield Your case?

Garfield No, no, his. It's Mr Smith's case, I'm taking it to him in the hospital.

Mrs Garfield It looks like a make-up case.

Garfield Does it? Well, it is.

Mrs Garfield (*horrified*) Mr Smith wears make-up?

Garfield Yes, I shouldn't say it, but he's a bit that way inclined. He should have gone to Brighton. So I'm taking his make-up case to him because he wants to look his best for the operation.

Mrs Garfield Wait a minute. If that's Mr Smith's case, what's he doing with the initials M.U. on it?

Garfield Er—well—ah! Those aren't his initials, it's M.U.—make-up.

Mrs Garfield That's ridiculous.

Garfield I know. He even puts his winter clothes in a case marked W.C. He's very eccentric.

Mrs Garfield He sounds it. I suppose that's his case as well. (*She points to Michele's case at the foot of the bed*)

Garfield (*pushing the case under the bed with his foot*) Yes it is. I'm taking that to him as well. I really ought to go and see him right away.

Mrs Garfield This won't take a moment. (*She continues winding wool*)

Garfield It might be my last. I mean, I'm going to be terribly busy from now on, what with one thing and another.

Mrs Garfield What a pity. We could have had a game tomorrow. I've got the morning free.

Garfield Quite impossible. But if you want to play by all means borrow my clubs. I shan't need them where I'm going to be.

Mrs Garfield Where are you going to be?

Garfield In bed—on the bed—the patient will be on the bed and I'll be on the patient—I mean I shall be operating on the patient . . . Would you like to borrow my clubs?

During this Garfield, in his anxiety to hurry the winding, lets go of three or four strands of wool which tangle up. He tries to disentangle it, putting one end of the skein over his head to free his hand

Mrs Garfield Thanks very much. The Manager told me one of the other guests is a golfer.

Garfield Oh really.

Mrs Garfield Yes. He's brought his clubs with him.

Mrs Garfield tries to help with the tangle and drops the ball of wool

Garfield Oh, that's very convenient.

Garfield picks up the ball of wool and in doing so steps over the running end by mistake

Mrs Garfield Yes. He's going to introduce us.

Garfield Oh, is he?

Mrs Garfield He must be keen.

Garfield I'm sure he is.

Mrs Garfield Yes. He was putting on the landing.

Garfield Putting on the landing? Oh my God.

He drops the ball of wool again. Through the next section they both become caught up in the wool and between them weave a tangled web

Mrs Garfield What's the matter?

Garfield Oh my God, he must be keen. But I don't think you ought to play with him.

Mrs Garfield Why ever not?

Garfield I've met him, and he only plays indoors.

Mrs Garfield Oh yes, I see what you mean. After all, he is on his honeymoon.

Garfield Is he really? I don't expect you will see much of him. In fact I'm sure you won't.

Mrs Garfield George, in a previous life I think you must have been a spider. A very clumsy one. With eight left feet. Give it to me, you're hopeless.

He bundles up the wool and gives it to her, but holds on to the ball. She tries to unravel the wool

Garfield Let's go down together and have some supper.

Mrs Garfield I'm not feeling hungry.

Garfield Oh but you must. The food here's absolutely marvellous. They're renowned for their cold sideboard.

Garfield ushers her out of Room 12a, shutting the door behind him

Mrs Garfield I find that very hard to believe.

Garfield Yes, isn't it. (*He pushes the lift button*)

The lift starts to come up

In Room 12a Michele comes out of the dressing-room and looks round for her case

Mrs Garfield You've forgotten Mr Smith's other case.
Garfield (*not sure what to do*) Er—yes.
Mrs Garfield Don't worry, I'll get it.
Garfield No. It's far too heavy for you. I'll get it.

He half opens the door of Room 12a, sees Michele who has her back to him, looking under bed for the case. He quickly shuts the door. Michele looks round, shrugs and pulls the case out

No I won't. I'll—er—get it later.

The lift arrives, he opens the doors

After you, my dear.

Mrs Garfield gets into the lift

Well, I must say I was rather dreading this week-end. But it's turned out so well now that you're here.

Garfield gets into the lift, closes the door, and drops the ball of wool outside the lift. The lift goes down. Albert comes out of Room 14, carrying his tools

Mrs Garfield (*off*) George, you've dropped it.
Garfield (*off, receding*) I couldn't help it. It slipped out of my hand.

Albert picks up the ball of wool, which bounces around in his hand as it unwinds and disappears down the lift shaft

Albert Come back 'ere. You've dropped a stitch.

Albert goes off by the upstage corridor

In Room 12a Michele takes a dress out of her case

Michele goes into the dressing-room to hang up her dress. Julie comes in from the bathroom, without hat and jacket, and carrying Clifford's pyjamas, which are very old-fashioned, and her nightdress, which is very demure

Julie puts the pyjamas on the bed and tucks her nightdress under the pillow

Julie goes back to the bathroom. Michele comes out of the dressing-room

Michele sees the pyjamas. She picks them up, aghast, and deposits them in the wastepaper-basket. She returns to her suitcase to complete her final bit of unpacking

Garfield, still carrying the make-up bag, rushes on from the upstage corridor and into Room 12a, closing the door

Garfield Thank goodness. There you are.
Michele You've been a long time.
Garfield I've been looking all over the place for you. You've got to move out of here. (*He puts the make-up bag down*)
Michele Move out! I've only just moved in.
Garfield They've put us in the wrong room. Mixed up the booking. You've got to move to another room.
Michele I don't want to move to another room. I like this one.
Garfield The other one is much better. The best they've got. Very large. Absolutely palatial. You'll be hidden away. No-one will see you there.
Michele I don't want to be hidden away.
Garfield But you must. She mustn't see you.
Michele What are you talking about? Who mustn't see me?
Garfield One of my patients. She's just arrived. She mustn't see you because she knows you're my patient too, and I could be struck off for doing what we haven't done yet.
Michele You mean we wouldn't be able to get married after your divorce?
Garfield Exactly. We wouldn't be able to afford it if I was struck off.
Michele Oh all right. I'd better pack my things. Which room are we moving to?
Garfield Which room? The Manager's busy sorting it out now.
Michele But you said he was giving us the best room.

The lift starts to come up

Garfield That's just it, he's trying to decide which is the best room. I'll go and help him make up his mind.

Garfield dashes out of Room 12a, closing the door, up the passage and off by the upstage corridor

Michele starts to pack her case

As Garfield disappears, Mrs Garfield comes out of the lift, leaving the doors open, followed by Albert

Albert I'm sorry about your wool, madam, but you shouldn't be knitting in our lift shaft. You could interfere with the machinery.
Mrs Garfield It's news to me it's got any. I thought it had a life of its own. I don't know what I'm going to do with this. (*She indicates the tangle of wool*)
Albert I could offer a suggestion.
Mrs Garfield Don't you dare. You can go and find my husband.
Albert I don't know anything about him. I'm surprised you've got one.
Mrs Garfield What? I'm surprised you're still in a job. Anyway as long as you are, you can go and look for him. He disappeared before we ever got to the dining-room.
Albert He's no fool. He must have eaten here before.

Mrs Garfield gives him the key to Room 18

Mrs Garfield You can start moving my things into this room.

Albert Not that harp again!
Mrs Garfield Get on with it. I'm moving in with my husband.
Albert But that's Mr Smith's room.
Mrs Garfield Yes, I know Mr Smith booked it, for my husband, before he went to hospital.
Albert Your husband's gone to hospital?
Mrs Garfield No, Mr Smith's gone to hospital.
Albert That didn't last long. Must have over-exerted himself.
Mrs Garfield No, gallstones.
Albert What did you say?
Mrs Garfield Gallstones. He's having an operation.
Albert Oh.
Mrs Garfield So I'm moving in here with my husband.
Albert He a musician as well? He's not the bloody pianist is he?
Mrs Garfield Don't be so cheeky. My husband is a doctor.
Albert Oh is he. That's handy. He might be able to give me something for all my allergies.
Mrs Garfield My husband has better things to do with his time. He's already given up his golfing week-end.
Albert (*muttering*) Well he can stick it.
Mrs Garfield What did you say?
Albert Does he play cricket?
Mrs Garfield He used to before his back gave out. What's it to do with you? Kindly move my things at once.

Mrs Garfield walks into the lift and goes down. Albert goes into Room 18, muttering

Albert With a mouth like hers she ought to play the harmonica.

In Room 12a, Michele goes into the dressing-room to fetch her dresses. Julie comes out of the bathroom, sees the french windows open and closes them. Albert comes out of Room 18 with Mrs Garfield's music case and stand and puts them outside the door of Room 12a. He goes back into Room 18 for the harp, leaving the door open

Julie comes out of Room 12a, shutting the door. She goes to the lift and pushes the button. The lift starts to come up. There are mutterings off from Albert, accompanied by discordant twangs and crashes

Albert emerges from Room 18 with the harp. He plonks it in the passage

Julie Oh! Is my husband still in the bar?
Albert No, madam. They've taken him to hospital.
Julie Hospital! I told him only to have one drink. He's got alcoholic poisoning.
Albert No, it's gallstones. They're going to operate. Cut them out.
Julie Operate. I must go to him. They mustn't cut anything out, we've only just got married. My poor Badger.

Julie hurries into the lift and goes down

Albert Badger? (*Calling after her*) No livestock allowed in the rooms.

Albert mutters again and goes into Room 18 to get Mrs Garfield's suitcase. Simultaneously, Michele comes out of the dressing-room with an armful of dresses: she sees the french windows are shut, so opens them again, then picks up her make-up case and goes into the bathroom, shutting the door. Clifford comes on by the upstage corridor and into Room 12a, closing the door behind him

Clifford Squirrel? (*He sees the open french windows, goes to them and calls*) Squirrel, are you out there?

Clifford goes on to the balcony and off opposite the upstage corridor side. Albert comes out of Room 18 with Mrs Garfield's case

Albert opens the door of Room 12a and puts the case inside the dressing-room and the music case and stand below the dressing-table. He leaves the door open. He picks up the harp and, muttering and cursing, struggles into Room 12a with it

This brings Michele out of the bathroom, lipstick in hand

Michele What do you think you're doing?
Albert Shifting this harp, what does it look as if I'm doing—driving a bus?
Michele You can't bring it in here, I haven't moved out yet.
Albert I'm not moving it back. It's playing hell with my allergies. Now I've got a new one—chronic Harpititis.
Michele Oh, really!

Michele goes into the bathroom, slamming the door behind her

Albert (*to the harp*) You stop there. I'm not moving you again tonight.

Albert goes out to the corridor, closing the door

Clifford comes in from the balcony

Clifford Squirrel! (*He sees the harp*) Oh! (*He goes to the telephone*)

In the corridor Albert moves upstage, turns and comes back

Albert No, I'll take the lift. Me feet's allergic to stairs.

The lift starts to come up. In Room 12a, Clifford speaks into the telephone

Clifford Oh, is that the Manager? . . . There seems to be a harp in my room. . . . Yes, a harp. I wonder if you could ask the porter to take it away? . . . You will? . . . Thank you very much. (*He puts down the telephone*)

In the corridor, Mrs Garfield gets out of the lift. She is carrying her knitting and knitting-bag separately

Mrs Garfield I hope you've moved it.
Albert Yes, I have.
Mrs Garfield Good. Now you can bring up my malted milk and biscuits.

Albert (*muttering*) Stupid cow!
Mrs Garfield What did you say?
Albert I'll do it now.

Albert gets into the lift, slams doors and goes down

Mrs Garfield goes into Room 12a. Clifford is examining the harp. He twangs it

Mrs Garfield Young man, what are you doing in my room?
Clifford Oh I'm terribly sorry. I thought it was mine. They're so much alike.
Mrs Garfield No, it was booked for my husband by his patient. He's having an operation in the morning, you know.
Clifford Oh, I see.
Mrs Garfield Yes, so I'm afraid you've made a mistake Mr whatever-your-name-is.
Clifford Smith.
Mrs Garfield Smith? Smith? Oh, then you're him. You poor man. I was so sorry to hear about your little problem.
Clifford Oh you've heard? I've only just found out about them myself. I didn't know they could be so violent. I'm going to get them to send up some more water.
Mrs Garfield That's right, plenty of liquids. But there's no need to worry.
Clifford Isn't there?
Mrs Garfield No, you won't know a thing about it.
Clifford Won't I?
Mrs Garfield No, you'll be asleep.
Clifford Will I? I'd much rather stay awake.
Mrs Garfield Oh, quite impossible in a case like this. Before you can count up to ten it'll all be over.
Clifford As quick as that. Oh my goodness.
Mrs Garfield Well there's one thing to be thankful for, at least you can afford to have it privately.
Clifford Yes, I wouldn't want it in public.
Mrs Garfield No, no, of course not, that's the joy of having a private room, all your gay friends can come and visit you whenever they like.
Clifford But I don't want my friends to come and visit me.
Mrs Garfield You feel like that now, but you'll be glad of them after you've been lying there for a few days. (*She puts her knitting on the end of the bed*)

Mrs Garfield comes out of Room 12a into the corridor. Clifford follows her anxiously

Clifford A few days? I can't stay in bed that long.
Mrs Garfield You'll have to. You'll find it takes a lot out of you.

She presses the lift button, the lift starts to come up

Clifford Oh dear, I didn't know that. You see, this is my first time.

Mrs Garfield And let's hope it's the last. It must be very painful when they're as big as golf balls.

Clifford What?!

Mrs Garfield Yes, that's why you've got to have the operation.

Clifford Operation?!

Mrs Garfield Yes, I'm afraid surgery's the only thing. You'll feel like a new man without them.

Clifford I shan't feel like a man at all. I feel faint.

Mrs Garfield Oh my goodness, they must be on the move. You stay in that room, you need a doctor. I'll go and fetch my husband. They'll put them in a jar for you if you like. You can see them when you wake up. (*She gets into the lift and closes the doors*)

Mrs Garfield goes down in the lift

Clifford I'm not staying here. She's a mad-woman. She's going to have me doctored.

Clifford runs back into Room 12a and out to the balcony, as Garfield comes on by the upstage corridor and goes into Room 12a. At the same time Michelle comes out of the bathroom

Garfield Haven't you packed yet? (*He sees the harp*) Good God, what's that?

Michele It's a harp.

Garfield I know that, but who brought it in here?

Michele The porter.

Garfield Just the porter? No-one else? I mean it's rather heavy for one man to carry on his own.

Michele Yes, he was on his own, and he wasn't very pleased about it.

Garfield Good. Hurry up, you've got to get out before she gets here.

The lift starts to come up

Michelle She?

Garfield Er—the lady harpist.

Michele How do you know she's a she?

Garfield Well I don't—but all lady harpists are shes.

Michele Yes, of course they are. I've just remembered, your wife's a harpist, isn't she?

Garfield Ah yes, but that's not her harp. And anyway she's miles away.

The lift doors open and Mrs Garfield comes out

Now quick, there isn't a moment to lose. I mean we don't want to lose a moment together.

Michele It's no good rushing me. I haven't finished packing yet and I'm in the middle of fixing my make-up.

Michele goes into the bathroom and shuts the door

Garfield Oh good grief!

Garfield grabs a handful of underwear and is about to put them in the case when Mrs Garfield enters Room 12a

Mrs Garfield There you are, George.
Garfield Oh hell . . . O Winifred!
Mrs Garfield I've been looking everywhere for you. (*She looks round*) Oh, he's gone!
Garfield Who's gone?
Mrs Garfield Your patient.
Garfield My patient?
Mrs Garfield What are you doing with that underwear?
Garfield Underwear? Oh this underwear. Er—packing—er—unpacking for you my dear.
Mrs Garfield (*taking a scanty bra from him and holding it up distastefully*) What's this?

Garfield drops the other underwear on top of the ball of wool on the bed and takes the bra from Mrs Garfield

Garfield It's a bra—you know, for supporting your . . .
Mrs Garfield My what?
Garfield (*looking at her*) Oh yes, I see what you mean. (*He puts the bra in the case, picks up the other underwear with the ball of wool and puts it all in the case, which he closes*) Ah, the porter must have mixed up the cases. Let's take it downstairs and find out what he's done with yours. (*He is about to pick up the case*)
Mrs Garfield Yes, all right then. You do that, and I'll have a quick wash. (*She goes to the bathroom door*)
Garfield No! (*He drops the case on the bed*)
Mrs Garfield (*turning*) What do you mean, no? My hands are filthy.
Garfield I mean there's no time, we haven't eaten yet. They'll close the dining-room.
Mrs Garfield I'll only be a minute. I'm not eating with dirty hands. (*She opens the bathroom door a few inches, turns to him and closes it again*) Anyway, before you think about your stomach, you want to do something about your patient. He's not at all well.
Garfield No, he's not, is he. I don't feel too well myself.
Mrs Garfield (*opening the bathroom door a crack and then closing it again*) What's the matter with you? Have you got gallstones as well? They'll have to make it a double operation.
Garfield No, no, just my nerves.
Mrs Garfield Oh well you'd better take one of my pink pills. That'll calm you down. (*She opens her handbag*)
Garfield (*shouts*) I don't want calming down! (*He controls himself*) I just want you to come downstairs with me and help me find my patient.
Mrs Garfield (*going to him*) Why on earth should I? I'm not your receptionist now you know.
Garfield No, but you could help me out, as Michele isn't here. Four eyes are better than two.

Mrs Garfield Who are you calling "four eyes"? (*She rummages in her bag for tablets*)

Michele comes out of the bathroom, sees Mrs Garfield, and freezes

Garfield tries to wave her to the french windows. Mrs Garfield finds the tablets, looks up at Garfield, and sees him waving

What are you doing?

Garfield Getting rid of the flies.

Mrs Garfield What flies? There's no flies in here. Your nerves must be bad, you're seeing things now. (*She looks round, sees Michele and does a double-take*) Miss Unsworth! Now I'm seeing things.

Michele comes down

What are you doing here?

Garfield Yes, what are you doing here?

Mrs Garfield I said that.

Garfield I thought you did.

Mrs Garfield Thought what?

Garfield What, what?

Mrs Garfield Said that.

Garfield Who did?

Mrs Garfield I did.

Garfield You did?

Mrs Garfield Shut up, I'm talking to her.

Michele Me?

Mrs Garfield You.

Garfield Her?

Mrs Garfield George, be quiet. I want to know why she's here.

Garfield So do I. Why are you here, Michele?

Michele You know why.

Mrs Garfield You know why?

Garfield I know why? I know why. (*To Michele*) Why?

Michele Er—well . . .

Mrs Garfield Don't bother. I know why you're both here. I see it all now. M.U.—make-up indeed! More like Michele Unsworth. I suppose you've got another case with D.W. on it.

Garfield D.W.?

Mrs Garfield Yes, Dirty Week-end. You can't fool me. I shall sue you for divorce, have you struck off, you—you—surgery seducer! (*She gets a pillow off the bed*)

Garfield No, no, you don't understand.

Mrs Garfield I understand all right. I'll belt you all the way to Bromley. I'll knock you into the North Sea. (*She belabours him with the pillow*)

Michele What's she doing here anyway?

Mrs Garfield (*rounding on her*) Don't you "she" me, or I'll start on you, you tall tart. How dare you come here with a married man.

Garfield Wait a minute. Why shouldn't she come here with a married man?

Mrs Garfield Married?! I'll have you for bigamy. (*To Michele*) How dare you marry my husband behind my back, under my very nose.

Garfield But she hasn't married *your* husband, she's married *her* husband.

Michele What?

Mrs Garfield Don't give me that. She wasn't married when I saw her yesterday.

Garfield No she wasn't, that's because she was only married today. And she's here on her honeymoon and that's why her husband's here with her—(*to Michele pointedly*)—isn't he?

Michele Is he?

Garfield Yes, they rang up a moment ago to say he's just arrived.

Mrs Garfield Just arrived? Why didn't they come down together?

Garfield He had to stay behind for a bit.

Mrs Garfield Stay behind for a bit? A bit of what?

Garfield A bit of work. He was working. He couldn't get away right away, because—because he's the registrar. That's it, she's married the registrar.

Michele Thank you very much.

Garfield Not at all. Sorry I couldn't be there to give you away.

Michele You've made up for it since.

Mrs Garfield Do you mean to say he was working on his wedding day?

Garfield Yes, he was.

Mrs Garfield How extraordinary. He married himself?

Garfield No, he married Michele. Oh, I see what you mean. Well, he had to at the last minute because the other registrar was taken ill. He had to marry lots of other people afterwards.

Mrs Garfield Oh I see. Well I suppose congratulations are in order, Miss Unsworth—I mean Mrs—Mrs—er . . .

Michele Er—er . . .

Garfield Smith. Mrs Smith.

Mrs Garfield Well, I can't wait to meet your husband.

Michele Neither can I!

Mrs Garfield I beg your pardon?

Garfield She can't wait to meet him again because they've been parted all day.

Mrs Garfield Do let me have a look at your wedding ring.

Michele But it's very ordinary. I'm sure you don't want to see it.

Mrs Garfield Oh, but I do. (*She takes Michele's hand and looks at the ring*) There's nothing ordinary about this ring. Look "G.G.".

Michele Yes, it's my Great Grandmother's.

Mrs Garfield It's my husband's. I should know, I gave it to him.

Garfield And I gave it to her—er—I lent it to her—because she hadn't got one of her own. It was all very sudden. She had to get married in a hurry.

Mrs Garfield Oh I see. It's like that, is it? You had to get married.

Michele No, no, I don't want you to think it's like that.

Mrs Garfield No I don't suppose you do. I can't say I approve, but I suppose one might have expected it.

Michele I didn't do anything.

Mrs Garfield I realize that. That's precisely why you're in your present condition.

The lift goes down

Garfield Come along, my dear. We'll go downstairs to reception and find out which room they're going to put us in—eh—put you and your husband in.

Garfield picks up Michele's case, goes to the door and opens it

Mrs Garfield I'll just wash my hands and I'll see you in the dining-room, George. (*She goes towards the bathroom*)

Garfield and Michele go into the corridor, closing the door

Michele I thought you said the Manager was giving us the best room.
Garfield Yes, he's doing his best. We're all doing our best. Come along.

Garfield and Michele go off by the upstage corridor

The wool unwinds as they go, unseen by Mrs Garfield in Room 12a. The knitting on the bed starts to move in jerks. It falls on the floor and slides towards the door. Mrs Garfield sees it and tries to catch it. She eventually does so, after several unsuccessful attempts

Mrs Garfield My bedsocks are on the march. Gotcher! (*She opens the door and sees the wool going off upstage*)

The lift starts to come up

George, come back. You're pulling my wool.

Mrs Garfield winds the wool as she goes off upstage. The lift doors open and Garfield and Michele come out. The end of the wool falls out of the suitcase. Garfield sees it as he closes the lift doors

Garfield We're being followed. My God—it's my wife's knitting. Quick, in there before it catches up with us.

The lift goes down

Michele How dare you tell all those lies about me to your wife! Why didn't you tell her the truth about us? I don't think you want to marry me at all.
Garfield Oh I do, I do. It's just because I do want to marry you I had to tell a few little white lies.
Michele White lies? You told her I was pregnant. I'm not pregnant.
Garfield Well we can soon put that right.
Michele (*shocked*) What?!
Garfield No, I mean we can soon put that right with my wife. I'll tell her it was a phantom pregnancy.
Michele Oh, I see. (*She moves towards Room 18*) I hope number Eighteen is a decent room.
Garfield Well, of course it is.

The lift starts to come up

Just stay in there and I'll come to you as soon as I can.

Michele Mind you bring some food with you. I'm not getting anything.

Michele goes into Room 18 and shuts the door

Garfield Neither am I. (*He sees the lift coming up*) Oh my God, she's picked up the trail!

Garfield goes off upstage. The lift doors open. Mrs Garfield comes out, still winding wool, and comes to the end of it in the passage. She picks up the end

Mrs Garfield Of all the times to run out of wool. Now where have they gone.

Clifford comes on along the downstage corridor

Clifford Oh dear, I'm lost again. Fourteen, Fifteen, Sixteen. Oh my goodness.

Mrs Garfield Ah!

Clifford Oh my golf balls!

Mrs Garfield Still on the move, are they? The doctor won't be long.

Clifford I don't want the doctor, I just want my room. I must find my Squirrel.

Mrs Garfield Oh dear. Delirium's setting in. There are no squirrels here.

Clifford Yes, Squirrel, my wife. I've lost my wife.

Mrs Garfield Your wife? You've got a wife?

Clifford Yes, it's rather awkward.

Mrs Garfield I'm sure it is, the way you are.

Clifford I didn't tell you before. But you see—(*he looks round to see no-one is about, then lowers his voice*)—I only got married today.

Mrs Garfield (*loudly*) Oh, you mean you're on your honeymoon.

Clifford Sssh!

Mrs Garfield No wonder you won't want to go to hospital. Good heavens, Mr Smith, of course, you're married to Mrs Smith.

Clifford Yes, I am.

Mrs Garfield My husband should have told me. I know your wife.

Clifford You know my wife?

Mrs Garfield I've just been speaking to her.

Clifford Have you? Do you know where she is?

Mrs Garfield Of course, she was at the end of this wool, with my husband, the doctor.

Clifford With the doctor, what's wrong with her?

Mrs Garfield There's no need to be coy with me, young man. I know all about her condition.

Clifford Did she tell you? It's very upsetting. Do you think it could be indigestion?

Mrs Garfield Don't be so naïve. Of course it isn't.

Clifford She can't help it you know. It happens every time anyone even mentions sex.

Mrs Garfield You mean this isn't the first time?

Clifford It keeps on happening to her. But she only told me about it tonight.

Mrs Garfield You poor man. It must be very difficult for you.

Clifford It's impossible. I don't see how we're going to get over it. I've waited so long for it, and now it's all spoilt.

Mrs Garfield You must have known what kind of girl she was when you married her.

Clifford Yes, I remember the first time I saw her, she looked so innocent amongst all those baby clothes.

Mrs Garfield Innocent! Hardly the word I would use. I'm afraid I've got to tell you that your wife is pregnant.

Clifford Pregnant! What? I can't believe it. I thought it was only hiccups.

Mrs Garfield Hiccups! Don't tell me you didn't know what you were doing when you did it.

Clifford But I haven't done it yet.

Mrs Garfield Your poor man. You're not even the father. Your wife's a nymphomaniac.

Clifford But she told me she'd never been out with anyone else.

Mrs Garfield She's a liar as well.

Clifford But she told me at the staff dance in the middle of the ladies' excuse me, "Badger," she said, "I'm saving myself all for you."

Mrs Garfield If you ask me she's the last of the big spenders. My advice to you, young man, is—be firm—assert yourself before it's too late. (*She opens the lift doors*)

Clifford Assert myself?

Mrs Garfield Yes, put her over your knee and give her a sound spanking, preferably with a cricket bat. That'll cure her. Your trouble is, you've spared the rod and she's got the child. (*She goes into the lift and closes the doors*)

Mrs Garfield goes down the lift

Clifford This is terrible. (*Nearly in tears*) Squirrel, how could you let anyone else nibble your nuts. (*He goes into Room 12a*)

Albert comes on upstage and down the corridor to Room 12a

Squirrel! Squirrel! Badger wants to talk to you. (*He goes up to the balcony*)

Albert knocks and enters

Is that you, Squirrel Nutkin?

Albert (*entering*) No, it's me, Yogi Bear. (*He goes to the harp and gives it a heave*) I've come for this perishing harp again.

Clifford Oh, I thought you were my wife. You see, I seem to have lost her.

Albert Yes, like that already is it? I've seen it so many times. Can't wait to get married—soon as they are they get frustrated. They see the grass is greener on the other side of the fence and before you know it, it's roll me over in pastures new.

Clifford Pastures new? So even you know all about it.
Albert Yes, I've seen it all. I remember we had one bloke here on his honeymoon, turned the light off to get undressed, never saw his wife again. She ran off into the night with the chef.
Clifford Oh, how terrible.
Albert Yes, it was. He was a good chef.
Clifford My wife wouldn't run off with the chef.
Albert Not with the one we've got now she wouldn't. He's a big pouf. Right, I'm taking this 'arp out of 'ere and I'm putting it in Number Eighteen and if they want it moved again, I won't be responsible for my allergies. (*He heaves the harp through the door*)
Clifford I can't stand any more of this. She's treated me like a worm. I'm going to end it all.
Albert What, you going to get a divorce?
Clifford No, I'm going to throw myself over the balcony. (*He goes out to the balcony*)
Albert Well, mind you don't land on the geraniums. (*He carries the harp out of Room 12a*)

Michele comes out of Room 18

Mind yerself. (*He goes towards Room 18*)
Michele What are you putting that in there for?
Albert Because the Manager told me to.
Michele Well, you can move it out again.
Albert I'm not moving it again unless the Manager tells me, and even then I mightn't.

Albert goes into Room 18 with the harp

Michele Oh, this is too much.

The lift starts to come up. Michele enters Room 12a, goes to the telephone and dials

Hello, is that reception? . . . Will you kindly tell the Manager to tell that horrible porter to move the harp out of Room Eighteen at once. . . . Thank you. (*She puts the telephone down*)

Michele goes into the bathroom. Albert comes out of Room 18 as Julie comes out of the lift

Julie You horrid old man. Frightening me like that. My husband isn't in the hospital.
Albert No, but he will be soon. He's just fallen in the geraniums.

Albert enters the lift and goes down. Michele comes out of the bathroom

Julie No, it can't be true. He's never done it before.

Michele comes out of Room 12a

Michele Good evening.
Julie (*baffled*) Good evening.

Michele goes into Room 18 and shuts the door. Clifford returns from the balcony

Clifford It's no use I can't do it.
Julie Badger! Badger! (*She enters Room 12a and sees Clifford*) Clifford Smith, what do you think you're playing at?
Clifford Oh, so you've decided to come back, have you.
Julie Yes, just as well I did. What's been going on? What was that woman doing in here?
Clifford What woman?
Julie You know very well what woman. I want to know what's been going on between you.
Clifford I don't know what you're talking about.
Julie Oh yes, you do. You've had another woman in here. I saw her coming out of the door.
Clifford I can only assume you've gone off your head. Due, no doubt, to the loose life you've been living.
Julie How dare you speak to me like that! Frightening me to death, telling everyone to say you've gone to hospital, and dropping dead in the geraniums, just so you can get up to horrid things behind my back. (*She starts to hiccup*)
Clifford Don't start that silly nonsense again. I know you're only putting it on to make a fool out of me.
Julie (*hic*) It's you who's making a fool out of me. (*Hic*, *Hic*) Mr Jenkins in Hardware was right. I should never have married you.
Clifford I suppose he was one of your many lovers.
Julie Lovers? (*Hic*)
Clifford Yes, along with Mr Hobbs of Sports and Games, Mr Mitchell of Garden Tools and Mr Wright of Bathroom Fittings. I wouldn't mind betting you've been right through the whole store, even poor old Mr Stone in Dispatch. No wonder he lost his trousers at the staff dance. I don't suppose you even know which one is the father.
Julie Father? (*Hic.*) Father of what?
Clifford Father of your next baby.
Julie (*hic*) You've gone mad! I've married a lunatic.
Clifford I've married a harlot! Very handy working in the Baby Department wasn't it. Probably helped yourself to clothes for all your babies.
Julie I'm going to call a doctor.

The lift starts to come up

Clifford You've already seen him. I know about that as well.
Julie I haven't. I haven't. I really haven't, Badger.
Clifford Please don't use that stupid expression—my name is Clifford. Although I have been shamefully deceived, I have married you for better or for worse, and things couldn't be any worse.
Julie (*hic*) No they couldn't.
Clifford However, from now on I am going to be firm, assert myself before it's too late. (*He advances towards her*)

Julie Keep away from me! (*Hic, hic*)
Clifford I'm going to put you over my knee and give you a good spanking!
Julie (*hic, hic*) Don't touch me!

The lift arrives. Albert comes out wheeling a trolley with champagne and sandwiches, decorated with lettuce and lemon wedges, on it

Clifford I'm going to show you who wears the trousers!

Clifford tries to get her over his knee, sitting on the bed. She struggles and they fall backwards on to the bed, still grappling with each other. Albert knocks, opens the door to Room 12a, and enters with the trolley

Albert Getting down to it, I see.

Clifford and Julie spring off either side of the bed and look very sheepish. Albert parks the trolley by the bedside table

Don't mind me. I'm quite used to it. Here's a bit of refreshment before round two. You can leave the tip on the trolley.

Albert goes out, shutting the door behind him, and off along the upstage corridor

Julie I'm not staying here with you a moment longer! I'm going home to Mother.
Clifford Good. And you can stop there. And if you see me in the Staff Canteen, don't speak to me because I won't answer.
Julie (*getting out her case*) If you eat in the Staff Canteen—I shall be taking sandwiches.

She goes into the bathroom and emerges with her hat and coat

Clifford I should eat them in the park. There's plenty of men there. You don't want to run short.
Julie You've put me off men for good. You and your women. (*She goes out, carrying the suitcase, slamming the door behind her. She opens the lift doors*)
Clifford Good riddance . . . ! (*With sudden realization*) Wait, you've got my clothes!

Clifford shoots out of Room 12a, slamming the door and arrives at the lift just as Julie bangs the doors shut. The lift starts to go down. As the lift goes down, Clifford talks to Julie going down on his knees gradually

Julie, I want my things. My sponge-bag. I've got to clean my teeth.

The lift, and Julie, have gone. Mr and Mrs Whiting come on by the upstage corridor and move down; they see Clifford on the floor. Douglas Whiting is a smartish, florid, rotund man. He carries a French horn case and a suitcase. He is panting. Evelyn Whiting is his scraggy, untidy-looking wife. She carries a handbag and a holdall that contains clinking bottles

It's my wife, she's run away with my toothbrush. I must catch her.

Clifford pushes past them and goes off by the upstage corridor

Douglas Mind where you're going. Pull yourself together. With the load you're carrying we should have waited for the lift. This must be Fourteen. Come on, Evelyn.

Evelyn There's no number on the door.

Douglas It's obvious. That's Eleven, that's Twelve and they never have a Thirteen, so this must be Fourteen. Follow me.

Douglas opens the door to Room 12a and walks in. She follows, closing the door behind her

Evelyn (*looking round*) Quite nice.

Douglas It's horrible. I told the Festival Organizer to find us a good hotel, and this is where he puts us.

Evelyn (*seeing the trolley*) At least they've left us some food.

Douglas That's a con trick. Don't touch that. I'm not paying for that. They can take that back. They should never have put me in this lousy hotel.

Evelyn You're always grumbling. Who do you think you are, Douglas Whiting, Yehudi Menuhin?

Douglas Don't be stupid. Yehudi doesn't play the French horn.

Evelyn No and his wife doesn't have to put up with those raspberry noises all the time.

Douglas gets out his French horn from its case

Oh, you're not going to blow it now.

Douglas I've got to practise for the opening concert tomorrow. Those factitious notes in the fourth horn passage in Beethoven's Ninth—I hate them.

Evelyn I like them. They always send me to sleep.

Douglas Well, don't snore in the front row like you did last year. They thought it was me playing bum notes. (*He blows a raspberry from his horn*) I think I've got a blockage. I'll go into the bathroom and clear it.

Douglas goes into the bathroom, taking his horn with him and shutting the door

Evelyn puts her holdall down with a pronounced chink. She opens it and takes out a bottle of Gordon's Gin. She looks around and puts it in the drawer in the bedside table. She takes out a second bottle and puts it under the bedclothes at the bottom of the bed. She takes a third bottle out, climbs on the bed and puts it inside the hanging bowl-lamp. She sees the carafe on the bedside table. She picks it up and empties the contents over the side of the balcony. She replaces it on the bedside table, takes out a fourth bottle of gin, opens it and places it upside down on the carafe, so that it empties itself. Whilst it is emptying, she takes out a fifth bottle and has a good swig. She puts the bottle back in the holdall, and goes to the telephone and picks it up

Evelyn Hello, Room Service . . . I'd like a small sherry. There's some sandwiches and champ . . . (*She takes the bottle and puts it under the bed*) There's sandwiches here, which we didn't order. Please take them away.

She replaces the telephone. Then she takes the now empty gin bottle off the carafe, bends down and puts it in the holdall. As she does so there is a French horn raspberry from the bathroom. She straightens up quickly, carries the clinking holdall to the dressing-room and puts it inside. There are a few loud notes from the French horn. Evelyn flinches. The lift starts to come up. She sits at the dressing-table and looks at herself in the mirror. She takes off her hat to reveal a quarter bottle of gin fixed to her hair. She drinks from it and goes out to the balcony

Evelyn goes out along the balcony away from the upstage corridor. The lift arrives. Julie comes out followed by Clifford, who is now carrying the case. They go into Room 12a

Julie You couldn't expect me to unpack my case in front of everybody Kindly take your things out and allow me to leave.

Clifford Don't worry, I'm not stopping you. (*He puts the case on the bed and starts to take out his things*) I shall be the laughing-stock of the Bedding Department. Fancy being married to a woman who pretends to have the hiccups every time I even mention the word sex.

Julie (*hic, hic*) I'm not pretending. (*Hic*)

Clifford Of course you are. I'll bet you didn't hiccup with all those other men, when you had sex with them.

Julie (*hic, hic, hic*) There weren't any—(*hic*)—other men. (*Hic*)

Clifford Don't give me that. You can't have babies without sex.

Julie Babies! (*Hic, hic, hic*)

Clifford And now there's another little . . .

Julie hiccups violently

(*Doing a take*) I do believe you're not pretending. You really have got hiccups.

Julie Of course I—(*hic*)—have.

Clifford Do you mean there weren't any other men?

Julie No there weren't. (*Hic*) I saved myself for you and—(*hic*)—look what I got as my—(*hic*)—reward. (*Hic*)

Clifford Oh, Squirrel, I knew I must be wrong about you. I never really believed it. Can you ever forgive me?

Julie No! (*Hic*)

Clifford Why not?

Julie You had that woman in *my* room in *my* bed—(*hic*)—on *my* honeymoon! (*Hic*)

Clifford There wasn't any woman. Do you want a glass of water?

Julie No, I want the truth.

Clifford I promise you, Squirrel, Scout's honour, I never saw any woman. I was out on the balcony.

Julie What were you doing out on the balcony?

Clifford I was so upset at losing you. I was going to throw myself over.

Julie Oh Badger, you'd do that for me?

Clifford Yes I would.

Julie But you didn't do it.

Clifford I know. I can't stand heights. But I'd do anything else for you, Squirrel.
Julie Anything?
Clifford Yes. Shall I get you a glass of water?
Julie It's all right, they've all gone now.
Clifford Oh, Squirrel.
Julie Oh, Badger.
Clifford Can I have a little nutkin?
Julie All right then, just a teeny nutkin.

They kiss chastely. French horn noises come from the bathroom. They jump apart in alarm

Oh! What was that?
Clifford It came from our bathroom. It must be the plumbing.

Another raspberry comes from the bathroom

Douglas (*off*) That's better!
Julie There's someone in there.
Clifford Leave it to me, Squirrel. Badger will flush him out.
Julie Oh, you are brave.
Clifford (*knocking timidly on the door*) Excuse me, would you mind coming out, sir, whoever you are?

Douglas comes out with his instrument in his hand

Douglas I haven't finished. I've only just cleared my instrument, I haven't started on my passage yet.
Clifford But that's our bathroom, you can't do that sort of thing in there.
Douglas Your bathroom? Don't talk rubbish, it's my bathroom. I'm not in the habit of blowing my horn in other people's bathrooms. What are you doing in my room?
Julie It's our room. We're in Twelve A.
Douglas Twelve A? I thought it was Fourteen. There's no number on the door.
Clifford I know. They haven't put it up yet, the porter told us.
Douglas Well, it's their fault then. Ruddy awful hotel. (*He picks up his case and horn case*) You like music, do you?
Clifford Oh—yes.
Douglas Good. I've got a couple of hours' practice to do. I shall only be next door, you'll be able to lie awake and enjoy it. (*He goes to the door*) Oh, she's wandered off I see. If my wife should stagger in, chuck her out and send her along to Fourteen, will you? Good-night.

Douglas goes out, shutting the door. He goes along the corridor, downstage and into Room 14

Julie I don't think I shall like listening to that all night.
Clifford (*putting case on the bed and opening it*) Never mind, you probably won't notice it when we're in bed.

Julie hiccups

Oh dear. Do try not to think about it.

Julie Yes, I will. (*Hic*)

Clifford (*taking out his dressing-gown*) It's time little furry animals were in their nests, Squirrel. (*He takes out a bra*)

Julie (*grabbing the bra and stuffing it back in the case. Hic, Hic*) I'll get ready—(*she grabs the case*)—in the bathroom.

Julie goes into the bathroom

Clifford Don't be long, Badger's getting—sleepy!

The lift goes down. Clifford looks round, sees his pyjamas in the waste-paper basket. He takes them out, grins, drops them back in

Oh, saucy Squirrel wants a bare Badger. (*During the following scene he quietly gets undressed, i.e. he takes off his shirt, socks and shoes, then puts on his dressing-gown before taking off his trousers*)

The lift comes up. The Manager and Albert come out. The Manager is carrying a small tray with a glass of sherry on it. Albert holds a grubby handkerchief to his nose

Manager Do put that filthy handkerchief away. It stinks. (*He takes his pocket spray out and sprays himself*)

Albert It's not the only thing. Next time I come in the lift with you I'll use the stairs.

Manager Don't be impertinent. It's all your fault there's been this terrible mix-up with the rooms. Get on with your work. Move that harp out of Eighteen at once. Mr Smith in Twelve A wants it.

Albert Last time I was up here he was getting it. Should be on round two by now. (*He goes to Room 18, knocks and enters*)

Michele (*off*) Oh!

Albert It's all right, madam, I've only come for the harp.

Albert goes into Room 18

Michele (*off*) Thank goodness, at last.

The Manager knocks on the door of Room 12a. Clifford, who has his trousers round his ankles, quickly whips them up again. N.B. He is wearing his dressing-gown. He goes to the door and opens it)

Manager My apologies, sir. I'm sorry for the unfortunate misunderstanding.

Clifford It's all right, thank you. We've sorted it out now.

Manager Oh good. One does like to think one has a good name, doesn't one.

Clifford I'm glad to say she has. She's not pregnant. She's not a nymphomaniac. There weren't any other babies, and the hiccups are real.

Manager I beg your pardon, sir?

Clifford And I haven't been having strange women in here.

Manager I'm very pleased to hear that. One doesn't like that sort of thing.

Clifford So I'm glad I didn't throw myself over the balcony.

Manager One wouldn't like that at all. That really would be blotting one's copy-book. I've brought your sherry, sir. I expect you need it.
Clifford Thank you very much.
Manager You see, sir, it was a double booking. I've had the other gentleman who was in here moved into Eighteen.
Clifford Oh dear. I sent him to Fourteen.
Manager That's Mr Whiting's room. I'll have to get him out of there at once. You won't be disturbed again. Good-night, sir.
Clifford Good night.

The Manager goes towards Room 14

Albert comes out of Room 18, carrying the harp, muttering

Clifford drinks the sherry, puts down the glass on the bedside table and starts to take his trousers off again. The Manager knocks on the door of Room 14. There is a horn raspberry

Manager Excuse me, sir. You've been directed to the wrong room. You should be in Number Eighteen. If I'd known you were brass I'd have put you in the annexe.
Douglas (*off*) Blast this hotel, it's run by idiots!

The Manager uses his cologne-stick and scurries back to the lift area, as Albert barges into Room 12a. Clifford, who has trousers round his ankles, quickly whips them up

Albert Oh, having a rest, are you?
Clifford What are you bringing that in here for?
Albert That's up to you isn't it. The Manager said to bring it. Is that round three then—doing it to music? (*He goes, shutting the door*)
Clifford I'll undress in here.

Clifford goes into the dressing-room

The Manager stands by the lift with the doors open

Manager Albert, everyone is complaining about the overpowering scent on this landing. I must do something about it.
Albert Why don't you go downstairs then?
Manager Don't be so insolent. Get an air-freshener and spray the landing.
Albert That won't do no good.
Manager Don't argue. Get in the lift.
Albert No thanks. I'll use the stairs. I haven't got my gas-mask with me.

Albert goes off along the upstage corridor. The Manager goes down in the lift. Julie peeps out of the bathroom door. She is now in bra and pants and holding a towel round her

Julie Clifford? (*Seeing no-one there, she comes into the room, goes to the bed, takes her nightdress out from under the pillow and puts it on over her bra and pants. She goes to the dressing-room door and taps on it*) Are you there, Badger?
Clifford (*off*) Shan't be a minute, Squirrel. I'm just taking my trousers off.

Julie gives a startled hiccup and runs off into the bathroom. The lift arrives and Mrs Garfield comes out. She carries her knitting. The ball of wool is now properly wound. She goes into Room 12a, leaving the door ajar

Mrs Garfield George? Now where's he gone? Well at least my harp's in the right place. (*She puts her knitting on the stool and gets her music-stand and music case. She puts the stand up, takes out what looks to be a piece of music, and puts it on the stand. She picks up her knitting, sits on the stool, impales the ball of wool on one of the spikes of the stand so that it revolves as she knits*)

Garfield comes in along the upstage corridor and knocks on the door of Room 18

Garfield Michele are you there?

Mrs Garfield hears his voice and gets up

Michele (*off*) Is that you George?

Mrs Garfield moves to the door of Room 12a taking her knitting with her, the ball of wool unwinding as she goes

Garfield Yes, can I come in?
Michele (*off*) I've got nothing on.
Garfield (*pleased*) Ah well in that case I will—
Mrs Garfield George.
Garfield —not come in.
Mrs Garfield I've been looking everywhere for you. Where have you been?
Garfield Er—I've been on to the Manager. The dining-room's locked.
Mrs Garfield I know that. What are you doing there?
Garfield Just making sure Michele's settled for the night.
Mrs Garfield (*pulling him into Room 12a and shutting the door*) Come in here. I want to talk to you about that girl. I've found out all about her.
Garfield You have? I promise you it's all lies, there's nothing in it.
Mrs Garfield Nothing in it? She's pregnant.
Garfield Oh is that all. I meant to tell you, it's a phantom pregnancy.
Mrs Garfield This one might be, but the others weren't.
Garfield Others?
Mrs Garfield She has them like shelling peas.
Garfield You mean Michele's got children?
Mrs Garfield Dozens as far as I can gather, and they've all got different fathers.
Garfield I can't believe it. It's not on her medical card. You must be going out of your mind.
Mrs Garfield It's not me, it's her. Do you know, she told her husband it was only hiccups, and she's saving herself for a badger.
Garfield You really must be ill. (*He takes her pulse*) You'd better lie down.
Mrs Garfield (*snatching her hand away*) There's nothing the matter with me. It's Michele you want to worry about.

The Manager comes on along the upstage corridor

Garfield I am worried about her.

The Manager knocks on the door of Room 12a

Mrs Garfield Come in.

The Manager enters

Manager Ah, Mr Smith, supper's ready.
Mrs Garfield What?
Garfield (*quickly*) Mr Smith's supper's ready. Mrs Smith's supper's ready. Everybody's supper's ready. Come along, Mrs Garfield.
Mrs Garfield What are you calling me Mrs Garfield for?
Garfield Well that's your name isn't it? (*To the Manager*) She's Mrs Garfield you know.
Manager Yes I know but . . .
Garfield (*quickly*) And I've invited her to supper.
Mrs Garfield It's disgraceful. You've no business locking the dining-room.
Manager I'm very sorry, I didn't know about it till Mr Smith told me.
Garfield No, I told you.
Manager That's what I said.
Garfield Yes so did I. Come along, my dear—my dear lady. (*He ushers her out of Room 12a on to the landing*)
Mrs Garfield What do you mean—dear lady?
Garfield Well you are a dear lady, dear. (*He opens the lift doors*)
Manager (*coming out of Room 12a*) But what about *Mrs* Smith?
Mrs Garfield Oh I wouldn't worry about her. She's behaved disgracefully and if he's taken my advice he's given her a sound thrashing. (*She goes into the lift*)
Garfield (*weakly*) Just a bit of fun between friends. (*He quickly gets into lift and closes doors*)

Dr and Mrs Garfield go down in the lift

The Manager looks baffled

Manager Wife-swapping on his honeymoon! (*He takes out his spray and sprays himself*)

Albert comes on along the upstage corridor with an aerosol can, spraying the landing. He goes past the Manager, pretending not to notice him, then bends down and sprays him through his legs

Albert! What are you doing?
Albert Getting rid of that smell like you told me.
Manager Where have you been? Nobody could get into the dining-room, the door was locked. Mrs Garfield was most annoyed.
Albert Dopey 'ore.
Manager What did you say?
Albert I'll open the door.
Manager Too late now, I've already done it.

The Manager goes off along the upstage corridor. Albert follows, spraying the Manager. In Room 12a, Evelyn Whiting, three-quarters of a bottle of gin the worse, and without her bottle, staggers on from the balcony

She picks up the empty sherry glass, snorts in disapproval and puts it down. She crosses over to the bed, gets in, right underneath the bed clothes head first, and rummages for her Gordons "hot water bottle"

Clifford comes in from the dressing-room, now in his dressing-gown only.

He sees a figure moving about in the bed

Clifford Oh, Squirrel has slipped in quietly has she? Well, Badger will slip in quietly beside her. We'll have a little frolic in the undergrowth.

Clifford slides quickly into the bed. After a moment Evelyn starts moving about. He reacts. The lift starts to come up.

Oh, naughty Squirrel. Squirrel has got cold paws. She must mind where she's putting them. (*He disappears under the bedclothes*)

Douglas comes out of Room 14, carrying his suitcase, French horn and case and goes into Room 18. Julie comes out of the bathroom, dressed in a demure nightdress. She carries her clothes, which she puts on the chair

Julie I'm ready, Badger.

Clifford immediately sits up in bed

Clifford Squirrel! I thought you were . . . Oh, Squirrel!

There is a scream from Room 18 and Michele runs out in a flimsy nightdress followed by Douglas. He remains in the passage baffled. She runs into Room 12a and out to the balcony

Michele There's a man with a horn in my room.

Albert comes on along the downstage corridor

As Michele runs through Evelyn sits up in bed

Evelyn I've found it. (*She produces the bottle of gin*)

Douglas runs into Room 12a, shutting the door behind him. Albert goes to door of Room 12a and peers through the keyhole

Julie (*aghast*) Badger! You beast!
Douglas My poor Evelyn!
(*Speaking together*)

Suddenly a bedspring shoots up between Clifford's legs like an Aristophenean phallus, making the bedclothes into a tent. N.B. This is a trick hand-prop bedspring. Julie, Evelyn and Douglas stare at it in horror

Clifford I told you, that always happens with an RT Seventeen. (*He pulls the spring out of the bedclothes*)

Julie runs into the bathroom and slams the door

Discordant music is heard, off, as—

the CURTAIN *falls*

ACT II

The same. A few moments later

The music continues as before. Dr and Mrs Garfield and Albert are getting into the lift. Julie is in the bathroom. Clifford is standing by the bathroom door. Evelyn is sitting up in bed nursing her gin, and Douglas has just entered. Michele has gone out on the balcony and is out of sight

The lift goes down

Clifford (*with the spring still in his hand*) Squirrel! Squirrel! Badger wants to talk to you.

Julie (*off*) Go away.

Douglas Listen here, you. How dare you take advantage of my wife in her condition.

Clifford I didn't know it was her. I thought it was my Squirrel.

Douglas Squirrel? How could you possibly mistake my wife for a squirrel? A battered old crow yes, but not a squirrel.

Evelyn What an extraordinary hotel. They've put gin in my hot water bottle. (*She takes a sip*)

Douglas Oh be quiet, Evelyn. (*To Clifford*) I'm still waiting for an explanation. You should be ashamed of yourself, leading my poor wife astray. Look at her, look at the pitiable state of her.

Evelyn He drank my sherry as well.

Douglas Shut up, you boozy old bat!

Evelyn He put his hand on my bottle.

Douglas What?! How dare you touch my wife's private things.

Clifford I can't understand it, that's the second time tonight there's been a strange woman in my room.

Douglas Oho! I know what you're up to. I've met your sort before. You're a pimp, that's what you are. Trying to get innocent young girls on the game. Well you're not getting my wife on the game.

Clifford I don't want your wife. I've got a lovely little wife of my own. At least I did have before you ruined everything. (*To Julie in the bathroom*) Squirrel, Squirrel, Badger wants to explain.

Julie (*off*) Go away!

Douglas Squirrel? Badger? He thinks he's an animal. He must be a raving drunk. Come along, Evelyn, I don't want you near him, it might be catching.

Evelyn He's a disgrace. Can't leave it alone. He drank my sherry you know.

Douglas (*pulling her out of bed*) Oh come on, before you start seeing the little green men.

Evelyn Yes, I don't like this room. It's full of beetles climbing up the wall.

Douglas (*at the door, to Clifford*) I've a good mind to give you a sound thrashing. And if I catch you with my wife again, I'll have your guts for violin strings. Anyway I'll make damn sure that sherry's on your bill.

Evelyn That's a good idea, let's have a sherry.

Douglas (*propelling her towards Room 18*) Get in there, you stupid old soak!

Douglas and Evelyn go into Room 18

Clifford (*going to the bathroom door*) Squirrel, please come out for Badger, they've all gone now.

Julie (*off*) You can go as well. I never want to see you again.

Clifford You don't understand. I thought it was your little paws running up and down me in the burrow.

Julie (*off*) Don't speak to me, you sex—(*hic*)—maniac.

Clifford I'm not a sex maniac. It's all a terrible mistake. Ask the Manager, he knows all about it. I'm going to fetch him, make him explain to you. (*He goes to the door*) I'll never be able to show my face in Bedroom Furniture again.

Clifford goes out along the upstage corridor. Douglas comes out of Room 18

Douglas All right, if it'll shut you up, I'll get your holdall.

Evelyn (*off*) It's in the little dressing-room. Be careful with it. I'm going on to the balcony to have a little—stroll.

Douglas knocks on the door to Room 12a. There is no reply, so he goes in

Michele comes on in the upstage corridor and goes into Room 18. Douglas sees there is no-one in Room 12a, and goes into the dressing-room. Michele comes out of Room 18 with a towel and sponge-bag and goes off to the bathroom, through the downstage corridor

The lift starts to come up

Julie opens the bathroom door, peeps out, sees nobody is there and comes out, still in her nightdress, to get her clothes from the chair. Douglas comes out of the dressing-room carrying the holdall. He sees Julie with her back to him and quickly goes back into the dressing-room. Julie takes her clothes into the bathroom and shuts the door. The lift doors open, and Dr and Mrs Garfield come out, go to the door of Room 12a and open it. At the same moment Douglas starts to emerge from the dressing-room. Douglas sees the door opening, and goes back in

Mrs Garfield What an absolutely disgusting meal.

Garfield I didn't think it was too bad.

Mrs Garfield (*entering Room 12a*) You wouldn't. You've got no taste. And what's more you've deceived me again.

Garfield How could I? I haven't had a chance yet. I mean . . .

Mrs Garfield Yes you did, about the food.

Garfield (*relieved*) Oh, the food.

Mrs Garfield Did you or did you not tell me this hotel was renowned for its cold sideboard?

Garfield Yes, I did.

Mrs Garfield Mildewed ham, soggy lettuce and rotting tomatoes.

Garfield I don't know. The wine was quite good.

Mrs Garfield Yes. Good for cleaning brass, I suppose.

Garfield Oh good heavens. I've left my cigarettes in the dining-room. I'll just pop down and fetch them. (*He starts to go*)

Mrs Garfield Oh, very well then. But hurry up. I must get a good night's sleep. I'm playing tomorrow.

Garfield goes into the corridor. He shuts the door behind him

Garfield Yes, and with a bit of luck I'm playing tonight. (*He takes a serviette out of his pocket, opens it out and reveals mushed up ham salad*) Doesn't look too bad to me.

Garfield goes into Room 18

Mrs Garfield starts to unzip her dress

Douglas, thinking the coast is clear, comes out of the dressing-room

He sees Mrs Garfield. He is about to return, when she turns and catches him.

She screams

Mrs Garfield Oh, how dare you, you filthy Peeping Tom!

Douglas (*crossing quickly to the door*) Please don't be alarmed. I was just getting my wife's things out of the dressing-room. (*He shakes the holdall —the bottles clink*)

Mrs Garfield Get out before I call the Manager!

Douglas comes out of Room 12a as Garfield comes out of Room 18. They turn and see each other

Douglas
Garfield } Wrong room. } (*Speaking together*)

They eye one another suspiciously and circle each other, as music starts, off

Douglas goes into Room 18. Garfield looks around for Michele—then goes off along the upstage corridor. Mrs Garfield goes into the dressing-room to get her case. Julie comes out of the bathroom carrying her case. She goes straight out of Room 12a to the lift. She opens the doors, gets in, and the lift goes down. Mrs Garfield comes out of the dressing-room and goes into the bathroom, shutting the door. At the same time Clifford, followed by the Manager come on along the upstage corridor. They both go into Room 12a

Clifford Please, you must explain to her. She's most upset. Refuses to understand about this woman in my bed.

Manager One hopes she's not still there.

Clifford (*as they enter Room 12a*) No, no, her husband took her away.

Clifford crosses to the bathroom door

Squirrel. The Manager's here. He's going to explain everything. Then it will be all right. Then we can go to bed.

The bathroom door opens and Mrs Garfield comes out in her petticoat, carrying her dress

Mrs Garfield I beg your pardon. (*She holds the dress up in front of her*)
Clifford Oh dear, it's you again—that's not my wife.
Manager We're well aware of that, sir. Might one suggest that one breaks the habit before one gets hooked.
Clifford No I don't make a habit of it. I've never even started.
Manager After all, this sort of thing must be very frustrating for your wife.

The lift starts to come up

Mrs Garfield I shouldn't worry about her. She's a raving nymphomaniac.
Manager Good gracious!
Clifford No she's not!
Mrs Garfield She's always having babies. She's pregnant again now.
Manager Pregnant? She can't have it in this hotel. It's a house rule: no children or dogs.

Julie comes out of the lift, leaving the doors open

Clifford No, no, you don't understand. She's really a very nice girl. And all I want to do is to spend the night alone with her.

Julie enters Room 12a

Julie I'm sure you do. As far as I'm concerned you can spend the rest of your life alone with her. I'm leaving.
Mrs Garfield Good heavens, he's got a girl with him.
Clifford You can't mean it. You've come back.
Julie I forgot my handbag.
Clifford (*trying to bar her way*) No, no. Please don't go.
Julie Out of my way—you bedding-department gigolo.

Julie sweeps out and goes into the lift, closing the doors in Clifford's face again

Clifford Squirrel. Squirrel! (*He goes back into Room 12a*) Look what you've done to my Squirrel.
Mrs Garfield Squirrel indeed. How dare you have the effrontery to bring her here on your honeymoon. You can see what sort of girl she is. It's written all over her face.
Clifford That's not fair. She's never done it before. Not ever. She's saved herself for me.
Mrs Garfield That's even worse. Seducing an innocent young virgin.
Clifford Yes, of course she's a virgin. I don't see what's wrong with that.
Mrs Garfield There, you see, no moral scruples at all. I wash my hands of you. I don't care if they get as big as footballs.

Clifford This is too much. It's making me feel bad. I think I'll go and be a monk. I might as well be.

Mrs Garfield Back to men again now, is it? You really are sick.

Manager Excuse me, if I might intercede. I'm afraid there's been a slight confusion with the bookings.

Mrs Garfield I'm not surprised in this rotten hotel. What's that awful common scent?

Clifford Yes, I noticed it coming up the stairs.

Manager I hadn't noticed anything. It really is most illusive. It seems to move about.

Mrs Garfield Now if you two men would kindly leave my room, I wish to go to bed.

Clifford But this is my room.

Mrs Garfield Don't talk rubbish. It's my room.

Manager I'm very sorry, madam, he's correct. I put you in Eighteen.

Mrs Garfield I know that, but that was before I knew my husband was here.

Manager I didn't know about that.

Mrs Garfield You don't seem to know much at all.

Manager I'm afraid I must ask you to remain in Eighteen.

Mrs Garfield I can't go in there with my husband. It's only a poky little single room.

Manager I can't help it, madam. It's the only room available. I have to put the other lady and gentleman in Room Twelve, because they did book a double room, and you only booked a single.

Mrs Garfield But what about my husband?

Manager If I may say so, you should have mentioned him before. I really must ask you to go to your own room.

Mrs Garfield Oh very well, I suppose I must. George will just have to sleep on the floor.

Mrs Garfield goes into the bathroom

Manager I must apologize, sir. I do hope you'll enjoy your honeymoon now.

Clifford How can I? My wife's gone.

Manager I'm sure she'll come back, sir. I have observed they are apt to get a little nervous on these occasions.

Clifford What if she doesn't come back?

Manager Well in that case, I still hope you'll enjoy your stay. At least you'll be able to have a nice rest.

Clifford I've had nothing to rest from yet.

Mrs Garfield comes out of the bathroom with her dress back on, and carrying her suitcase

Manager This way, madam.

Mrs Garfield (*giving the Manager her case*) Take that. My music case and my husband's things are in the dressing-room and see that my harp's moved at once. It's not safe in here with him.

Manager Of course, madam. (*He gets the case and golf bag out of the dressing-room*)

Mrs Garfield (*to Clifford*) I shall speak to your wife. It's high time she knew all about you. You're not even safe with men. (*She sweeps out into the corridor*)

Manager Just one thing, sir, if your wife should leave you for good, I'm afraid we shall still have to charge you the full double rate. (*He goes out, shutting the door*)

Clifford I feel sick.

Clifford goes into the bathroom

Manager (*to Mrs Garfield*) Allow me, madam. (*He has his hand on the door handle when a series of French horn notes sound in Room 18*) Good gracious, what's that?

Mrs Garfield It's a French horn in F. What do you think it is?

Manager But what's it doing in there?

Music starts, off

Mrs Garfield Tuning up by the sound of it, like all the others.

Manager But it shouldn't be in your room.

Mrs Garfield Exactly. I suppose with your usual efficiency you've booked the entire Festival orchestra into my room.

Manager Oh no, I assure you we haven't.

Mrs Garfield Well, get it out at once. I'm not having brass in my wardrobe, fiddles in my bed and woodwind in my drawers.

Music stops

Manager Yes, madam, at once. (*He knocks on the door of Room 18*) Excuse me, this is the Manager here. You're in the wrong room.

A raspberry is blown, off, echoed by the other musicians

Douglas bursts out of Room 18, in trousers and shirt

Douglas What do you mean, you fool, we're in the wrong room?

Mrs Garfield It's you, you Peeping Tom. Get out of my room!

Douglas What are you talking about, it's my room? He told me to come in here when I was in Fourteen.

Manager No I didn't. I told the other gentleman to come in here. But that was wrong. I should have put him in Twelve.

Douglas You don't know what you're doing, do you?

Manager Yes I do, sir.

Douglas Well, where am I then?

Manager I don't know, sir. I don't even know who you are.

Douglas I'm Whiting, you fool.

Manager Oh Mr Whiting. You and your wife should be in Fourteen.

Douglas Well why did you move us out, then?

Manager I didn't know it was you at the time. I thought you were Mr Smith.

Douglas Well I'm not.

Douglas goes into Room 18. The Manager follows in, puts down the luggage and returns

Mrs Garfield Kindly inform my husband that you have made us move to this dreadful little room.

Manager Yes, madam. Where is he?

Mrs Garfield He's gone downstairs for his cigarettes. Hurry up or you'll miss him.

Douglas comes out of Room 18 carrying his jacket, his French horn and the suitcase, followed by Evelyn who is now in her nightdress and who carries her holdall, and her clothes

Douglas (*thrusting the case at the Manager*) *You can carry that.*

Manager Yes, sir. Certainly, sir. May I take madam's bag as well?

Evelyn No, don't you touch that. It's got all my valuables in it. (*She sniffs*) What's that horrid smell?

Manager Oh dear, not you, too.

Evelyn No, it's not me. It's cheap scent. Douglas, that woman's got cheap scent on.

Mrs Garfield What?! How dare you!

Douglas Oh, it's you is it? Don't you ever wash?

Mrs Garfield Don't be so rude. You're drunk, you're both drunk!

Mrs Garfield goes into Room 18 and slams the door

Douglas Who's she calling drunk?

Evelyn Exactly. I am as sober as a judge. (*She staggers slightly*) Will you bring me a sherry. The last one I drank was drunked before I drinked it.

Douglas Yes, and we're not paying for it.

Manager This way, if you please.

He goes along the downstage corridor, followed by the Whitings

I think you'll find this room much more to your liking. It's one of our balcony rooms and very quiet.

Evelyn goes into Room 14

Douglas Don't take any notice of her, she's a bit Mozart and Liszt.

Manager Ah Liszt. Madam and I obviously have similar tastes.

Douglas You as well? You want to lay off it. No wonder you get the rooms mixed up.

Douglas goes off into Room 14. The Manager goes off along the upstage corridor

The lift starts to come up. Music starts, off

Garfield comes out of the lift, goes to the door of Room 18 and knocks on it quietly

Garfield (*calling softly*) It's me. Are you there? I've got some food. Can I come in? (*He takes out the serviette*)

Mrs Garfield opens the door and comes out in her nightdress

Mrs Garfield What are you knocking for?

Garfield Good God, it's you!

Mrs Garfield What are you doing with that food?

Garfield Er—it was so nice I thought I'd get some more in case we get peckish in the night.

Mrs Garfield Well, you're not having a nibble in my bed.

Garfield What are you doing in there?

Mrs Garfield They've messed things up again. This is our room now.

Garfield Oh, I didn't know that.

Mrs Garfield Then what were you knocking on the door for?

Garfield I'm looking for Michele, to make sure her husband's arrived safely.

Mrs Garfield He has. I've already told you. I've been talking to him.

Garfield You have? That's impossible. How could you?

Mrs Garfield It was very hard, I can tell you. Most peculiar young man, and he's thoroughly depraved. He deserves to be ill.

Garfield Does he?

Mrs Garfield Yes. I'd like to get at him with a scalpel.

Garfield Whatever for?

Mrs Garfield Obviously you don't know him very well.

Garfield No I don't. I'd like to, though.

Mrs Garfield No you wouldn't. You'd have a surprise.

Garfield I've already had one. I mean it was a surprise to me to find out that he's like whatever he is like. What is he like?

Mrs Garfield A nasty piece of work. I caught him with another girl, and he goes after men as well.

Garfield You mean you've met him and he's staying with Michele at this hotel?

Mrs Garfield Well of course he is, he's your patient.

Garfield My patient?

Mrs Garfield You told me so yourself.

Garfield Did I?

Mrs Garfield Yes, your patient, Mr Smith.

Garfield Oh, that Mr Smith. I see what you mean. I don't understand what's going on here.

Mrs Garfield I do. He's made Michele pregnant.

Garfield What?! Are you sure?

Mrs Garfield Quite sure. I think you ought to talk to her.

Garfield I will. I certainly will. I'll do it now.

Mrs Garfield We can't do it now. They're probably in bed.

Garfield My God. She's got a nerve. I can hardly believe it. I need a drink. (*He opens the lift doors*)

Mrs Garfield Oh, very well. While you're down there, find out what they've done with my malted milk.

Garfield shuts the doors and the lift goes down. Michele returns from the bathroom

Ah there you are, Michele. My husband and I were just talking about you.

Michele Were you really?

Mrs Garfield Yes, we were. It's all come out now. It's a pity he didn't tell me about you before, I might have been able to stop it.

Michele I know. I asked him to bring me here, but I didn't think it would turn out like this.

Mrs Garfield Well, presumably you knew what you were doing. It's pretty sordid.

Michele Yes I'm sorry. I'm rather ashamed.

Mrs Garfield Well we've got to be adult about it. I think a divorce is the best answer, don't you?

Michele Yes, I do. You don't mind?

Mrs Garfield No, I'm absolutely delighted. There's plenty of evidence. I know he's got another woman here, and I can tell you he's a practising homosexual.

Michele What? I can't believe it. How did you find out?

Mrs Garfield He told me.

Michele Who told you?

Mrs Garfield My husband of course.

Michele He never told me.

Mrs Garfield He couldn't. He only found out himself today.

Michele If I'd known that I'd never have come here with him.

Mrs Garfield Well don't let it worry you, my dear. My husband will talk to you about it in the morning. He'll get everything sorted out.

Michele You're very understanding.

Mrs Garfield I'm extremely sorry for you. You get a good night's sleep. And if he tries anything in the night, call me. I'm just across the corridor here in Eighteen.

Michele You're in Eighteen? But I'm in Eighteen.

Mrs Garfield No, no, this wretched hotel's got everything wrong again. You're supposed to be in Twelve A.

Michele But I don't understand . . .

Mrs Garfield That's British hotels for you. Still you're lucky. At least Twelve A resembles a room.

Michele I've left all my things in there.

Mrs Garfield I wondered whose they were. Do please go in and get them, my dear. I'm going to find out what that wretched porter's done with my harp.

Michele goes into Room 18

Mrs Garfield goes into Room 12a

Oh, that porter's useless. (*She caresses the harp*) At last I can get in a bit of practice. (*She gets her music stand and puts it up. She extends the top part which collapses sideways like two semaphore arms. She reverses the wings which then stay in place. She gets a piece of music from her music case and puts it on the stand. As she turns away the top of the stand flops down. She re-erects it and screws it up. She returns to the stool and rests the harp against her shoulder. It is the wrong way round, and will not stand up properly. She realizes, and turns the harp the right way round and settles it against her shoulder. She peers at the music and wiggles her fingers*) Knit one, purl one, knit two together. Oh, I am daft. (*She gets up, takes the knitting-pattern off the stand, gets out a piece of manuscript music which consists of several pages stuck together like a concertina. She discovers the concertina-like properties of the music and "plays" it. She sings*) "Sweet Adeline". (*She puts the music on the stand and returns to the stool. At that moment, the stand slowly subsides, the top section telescopes into the body and then the three legs splay out. She looks amazed. She goes to the stand and re-erects it. It stays upright. She returns to the harp. Whilst her back is turned, the stand subsides, this time more quickly. She turns, sees it, and does a double-take. She puts the stand up again, and this time tries to catch it out as she goes back to the harp. It does not move. Happily she prepares to play. The stand suddenly collapses again. Furious, she rises, rolls up her sleeves and advances upon the stand, which now slowly rises and resumes a proper stance. Delighted, she goes to the harp and plays the first phrase of "Colonel Bogey". The last two notes go sour. N.B. This is a trick music stand*) It's been got at!

Clifford comes out of the bathroom in his trousers and pyjama top

Clifford (*coming out*) Is that you, Squirrel? Oh, it's you.

Mrs Garfield Young man, what have you been doing to my harp?

Clifford Nothing.

Mrs Garfield You're not content with seducing men and women, are you? Now you've interfered with my harp again. Is nothing sacred.

Clifford You don't understand. I was in the bathroom.

Mrs Garfield How dare you take it in there. I suppose you've been playing with it in the bath.

Clifford No, no, I haven't been playing with anything in the bath.

Mrs Garfield examines the harp

Mrs Garfield Just as well for you. I might have got rising damp in my pedal-box. (*She picks up the house telephone and dials*) I've just been speaking to your wife.

Clifford You have?

Mrs Garfield (*into the telephone*) Hullo. Is that the receptionist? . . . Kindly have my harp moved into Eighteen at once. (*She puts the receiver down*) She's going to spend the night in here.

Clifford The receptionist?

Mrs Garfield Yes, you'd like that, wouldn't you?

Clifford No, I wouldn't.

Mrs Garfield Well, you're going to be disappointed. Your wife's coming in here tonight.

Clifford Oh, that's wonderful.

Mrs Garfield Only because she's got nowhere else to go. But remember, young man, I shall be across the corridor. You'll have me to deal with if you so much as lay a finger on her.

Clifford But it's my wedding night. I've got to. How can I do it if I don't? Oh dear, I never knew honeymoons were so complicated.

Mrs Garfield You should have thought of that before you sank into your sexual cess-pit. Good night, Dr Jekyll! (*She goes out to the corridor and shuts the door*)

Clifford But—but I'm not the doctor—oh dear.

Clifford goes into the bathroom and shuts the door

Mrs Garfield opens the door to Room 18

Mrs Garfield (*going in*) I've just spoken to him, my dear, he won't come near you tonight.

Mrs Garfield goes into Room 18 and shuts the door

Music starts, off

The Manager comes on along the upstage corridor and crosses downstage to Room 14. He carries a glass of sherry on a tray. He knocks on the door

The lift starts to come up

After a moment the door to Room 14 opens six inches and Evelyn's hand comes out and whips the sherry glass in. Almost immediately her hand comes out with the empty glass, which she puts on the tray and closes the door

The Manager reacts in disbelief, then goes back towards the lift

Michele comes out of Room 18 with her clothes, suitcase and make-up case, goes into Room 12a and shuts the door. She sees the sandwiches on the trolley and takes one. As the Manager reaches the lift, Julie steps out of it, leaving the doors open

Michele Oh, food. Smoked salmon. Ugh! mouldy bread! (*She puts it back on the plate, switches out the light, gets into bed and goes to sleep*)

Manager Oh, I'm glad to see madam's decided to return. One always feels that a honeymoon goes so much better when both parties are present.

Julie I've only come back because I've missed the last train to London. (*She sniffs*) Oo, what a nasty smell.

Manager I'm terribly sorry about that, madam. It's the lady in Eighteen. I fear she indulges in rather cheap scent.

Julie Oh, how awful. I'd like to have another room, please.

Manager I'm afraid we haven't got any. One is happy to say the hotel is full.

Julie Oh dear what shall I do?

Manager I can only suggest that you make it up with your husband.

Julie I'm never going to speak to him again. And I'm certainly not getting into bed with him. (*Hic, hic, hic*) I shall—(*hic*)—make him sleep in the —(*hic*)—bathroom.

Manager Oh very well, if you wish, madam. But I must ask you not to put any bedding in the bath. The cold tap drips. I wish you a good night, madam.

The Manager goes out along the upstage corridor

Julie goes into the lift, gets her case out and closes the lift gate and doors

Simultaneously in Room 12a, Clifford comes out of the bathroom in his pyjamas. He sees the figure in the bed

Clifford (*quietly*) Oh, lucky, lucky Badger, Squirrel's come back to our nest, and she's in the land of Nod. I'd better not wake her. I don't mind waiting till the morning.

He quietly slips into bed next to Michelle. Julie comes into Room 12a and switches the lights on. Clifford and Michele sit up in bed immediately. Julie screams

Michele Who's that?
Clifford Squirrel!
Julie You beast! You've got another one.

Clifford and Michele jump out of bed

The door to Room 18 opens; Mrs Garfield rushes out and into Room 12a

Michele What are you doing in my bed?
Clifford What are you doing in mine?
Julie I know what you're both doing and it's beastly. (*Hic, hic, hic*)

Julie runs into the bathroom and slams the door

Mrs Garfield (*seeing her go*) Two women on your honeymoon at the same time! One in the bathroom and one in the bed! Is there no end to your excesses?
Clifford But I haven't done anything.
Mrs Garfield No, I was just in time to stop you wasn't I? How dare you treat her like this.
Michele Yes, attacking me in my sleep.
Mrs Garfield (*to Michelle*) You come along with me, my dear. You'll be safe in my room. I'd like to see him try anything on with me.
Clifford I only want my wife.
Mrs Garfield You're not going to get her. Anything you get will come from our lawyers.

Michele and Mrs Garfield go out of Room 12a

Michele But what about your husband?
Mrs Garfield Don't worry about him, he'll understand. He'd want me to protect you.
Michele You really are very kind.
Mrs Garfield Think nothing of it.

Michele and Mrs Garfield go into Room 18

Clifford goes to the bathroom door

Clifford Squirrel, Squirrel, I didn't know there was a cuckoo in our nest.

There is no reply

I wasn't doing anything. I was going to wait until the morning.

Still no reply

That was before I knew it wasn't you. If I'd known it was her I'd have woken her up straight away. I mean—I mean I don't mean—I don't know what I mean. Please come out. Oh dear, I don't feel well. Where did you put the aspirins? Oh, I'll have to look. (*He goes to the bedside table. Opens the drawer and pulls out the bottle of gin*) How did that get there? (*He puts it back in the drawer and closes it. He starts to move away then thinks better of it. He gets the gin out again and sits on the bed*) Just a little one, I need something. I've had a terrible shock. (*He pours a small gin into the glass*) This is something else I've never had before. I wonder what it's like. (*He takes a sip and splutters*) Oh, it is strong. I'd better have some water with it. (*He sees the carafe and pours a good measure of the contents into the glass. He takes another sip*) That's a bit better. But it's still very strong. (*He fills the glass up from the carafe. He takes another sip*) That's fine. Won't do me any harm. (*He drinks the lot. Stands up swaying. He tries to put the glass down, but can't find the bedside table. He eventually manages to put the glass down, using both hands*)

The lift starts to come up. Clifford meanwhile has considerable difficulty getting into bed. Eventually he manages to get in the right way round, with the bedclothes completely covering him. He starts to snore

Garfield comes out of the lift

Garfield Wretched girl, Michele. What does she think she's playing at. I'll never find her now. Just as well, my back's killing me.

At the same time Albert comes along the upstage corridor carrying a tray on which is a glass of malted milk and a plate with two cream crackers

Music starts, off

Albert They must be lousy musicians if they have to practise all night. (*He goes to open the door to Room 12a*)

Garfield Ah! Is that my wife's malted milk?

Albert Yes. I'm just takin' it in to her, in' I?

Garfield You're taking it to the wrong room, man. She's with me in Eighteen.

Albert Oh no, she ain't. She's in there with her 'arp and I should know 'cos I done the shifting of it.

Garfield Oh good heavens, they've moved us again. A gypsy stays in one place longer than I do in this hotel.

Albert Wait a minute, you're a doctor aren't you, Doctor?

Garfield Yes.

Albert Well then, it's about these allergies what I've got. I think you ought to have a look at them. You can give me a bit of free advice.

Garfield Does your baker give you free bread?
Albert No. I can't eat bread, I'm allergic to it.
Garfield Too bad. Give me that, I'm going to bed. (*He takes the tray*) Oh and you can bring me up a large whisky.
Albert (*muttering*) Up your kilt!
Garfield What did you say?
Albert It'll get spilt.
Garfield You want to watch that and don't be so impertinent, or I'll plant my metatarsals up your coccyx. (*He goes into Room 12a*)
Albert It's not right a doctor using language like that. He ought to be struck off.

Albert goes off along the upstage corridor

Garfield Your malted milk.

Clifford snores

Too late.

Garfield puts the tray down, takes his coat off and looks around for his pyjamas

Where did she put my pyjamas?

A snore from Clifford. Garfield starts to undress during the following. He goes down to green pants and string vest

Stupid woman. I hate sleeping in my underclothes.

There is more snoring from Clifford

For God's sake stop that row. You should have your adenoids out. And I'd like to perform the operation myself. (*He goes over to the bed, and gets in beside Clifford*)
Manager (*off in the upstage corridor*) Will you do as you're told. Albert, put that harp into Eighteen at once.
Albert (*off*) I know where I'd like to put it, and you'd know all about it.
Manager (*off, sharply*) That's enough, Albert.
Garfield (*putting pieces of torn-up serviette in his ears*) I don't know how I've put up with it. Twenty-five years sleeping with a traction engine.

Albert comes in upstage, muttering, goes to the door of Room 12a, knocks and enters, leaving the door open

Albert I've come for the old bag's 'arp.
Garfield (*sitting up*) What the blazes do you mean by barging in here. (*Shouting*) Get out!
Clifford (*sitting up, drunkenly*) Oh, Squirrel. Don't make me wait till morning. (*He puts his arms round Garfield*)

Mrs Garfield comes out of Room 18, followed by Michelle

Garfield (*shouting*) Get off! Get off! (*He tries to free himself*)
Albert Blimey! A couple of nancys. We don't like your sort in our 'otel.

Mrs Garfield (*entering*) What's going on in here? Good gracious, he's attacking my husband now. Get him off!
Clifford Please be my little Squirrel.
Michele You were right, Mrs Garfield. He's thoroughly perverted.

Julie enters from the bathroom

Julie Clifford! What are you doing in my bed with that man? (*Hic, hic*)

Clifford releases Garfield, who gets out of bed

Clifford I thought he was you, Squirrel, and I didn't want to wait till the morning. (*He gets out of bed and staggers*)

Garfield wraps the eiderdown round himself

Julie Oh, you monster! You're drunk!

Julie goes into the bathroom and slams the door

Clifford (*staggering and hanging on to Albert for support*) She's left me. Badger wants his Squirrel.
Albert You're not having my Squirrel. Get off! (*He pushes him away*)

Clifford collapses in the chair

Mrs Garfield Porter. Get the Manager at once.
Albert (*muttering*) Get stuffed.
Mrs Garfield What did you say?
Albert I'm dead puffed—shifting this flamin' harp. Anyway he's gone to his bed out of it.
Mrs Garfield Has he, indeed. I shall get him up at once.
Michele Good idea.

Albert drags the harp out into the corridor and into Room 18

Mrs Garfield picks up the house telephone and dials

Mrs Garfield What's his number? Here we are—Manager: Four. (*She bellows into telephone*) Hullo! Hullo! . . . Well, you're very lucky, my man, we're getting no sleep at all. You must come up here at once. My husband has been assaulted by a homosexual madman. You heard what I said. He's competely nuts.

Clifford gets up uncertainly

Clifford Nuts—I haven't had any nuts yet. (*He sinks back into his chair*)
Mrs Garfield Be quiet, you. George, don't just stand there. Get some clothes on at once, you look ridiculous.
Garfield I couldn't find my pyjamas—where did you put them?
Mrs Garfield They're in Room Eighteen of course.
Garfield Stupid place to put them. (*He starts to go out, crossing Michele as he does so. To Michele*) I want to see you later, about the patient. He's very sick.
Michele He's not the only one. Pity you only found out about yourself this morning.

Garfield I don't know what you mean.
Mrs Garfield For goodness sake go and put your pyjamas on. You look like a string bag full of sprouts.

Garfield goes into the corridor

Albert emerges from Room 18

Garfield almost collides with Albert, who gives him a wide berth

Garfield Mind out.
Albert I will, don't worry. (*To himself*) I've met your sort before.

Garfield goes into Room 18

Albert goes into Room 12a. The lift starts to come up

I've moved the harp, madam. (*He puts out his hand to Mrs Garfield*)
Mrs Garfield It's no good putting out your hand. I'm not going to tip you any more.
Albert (*muttering*) Rotten bitch.
Mrs Garfield What did you say?
Albert I've got an itch. Must be my allergy.

Music starts, off

Blimey, they've started again. No wonder Beethoven went deaf.

The Manager comes out of the lift and into Room 12a. He's in his dressing-gown

Manager Albert what is going on? What are you shouting for?
Albert I'm shouting because I can't hear meself think.
Manager Well, be quiet about it. (*To Mrs Garfield*) Oh, there you are, madam. What seems to be the trouble.

Albert edges away from the Manager

Albert Cor, talk about a poof's palace.
Mrs Garfield You should be ashamed of yourself. This hotel is nothing more than a den of vice. (*Indicating Clifford*) This disgusting creature should be arrested at once. He seduced my husband.

Clifford gets up, trying to be dignified, but swaying

Clifford Madam. I never produced your husband. I'm not standing here to listen to your ins—ins—ins—rude remarks. I'm going to leave this hotel at once. (*He walks into the dressing-room*)
Mrs Garfield It's completely insane. You never know what he's going to do next.
Clifford (*coming out*) You've blocked up the corridor. I want to go.
Manager Not before you've settled your account, sir. Albert, take this gentleman downstairs and present him with his bill at once.
Albert Very good, sir. And I shan't forget the service charge. This way, you.

Clifford gathers up his clothes from the chair and follows Albert out. He goes towards the lift

Oh no, I'm not going in there with you. We're going by the back stairs —very appropriate in your case.

Albert and Clifford go off along the upstage corridor

Manager Now that's settled perhaps one can get some sleep.
Mrs Garfield Yes, now that awful man's gone.
Michele He gives me the creeps. I think he'd get into bed with anyone.
Mrs Garfield You behaved with great dignity, my dear. You were absolutely right to ignore him and treat him like a total stranger.
Michele He is a total stranger.
Mrs Garfield That's it. That's the way. Put him out of your mind. That scent's back. I can smell that cheap scent again.
Michele So can I. Isn't it awful?
Manager I can't smell anything.
Mrs Garfield It's stronger than ever.
Manager Excuse my mentioning it, but the remedy is in your own hands, or should I say handbag. Does madam know where the bathroom is?
Mrs Garfield Of course I do, and there's somebody in there. (*She knocks on the bathroom door*) Young woman, come out of there at once.

Julie comes out of the bathroom, fully dressed again and carrying her cases

Julie Excuse me, I'm leaving. I'm going to wait at the station for the first train.
Manager That's all right, madam. Mr Smith has paid the bill.
Julie I'm not interested in what Mr Smith does any more.
Mrs Garfield Glad you've come to your senses. You should never have come here tonight.
Julie No, I know I shouldn't. I ought to have known what he'd be like. It's all those beds, they've gone to his head. (*She goes out into the corridor*)

Garfield comes out of Room 18, with his sponge-bag and wearing his dressing-gown

Garfield Good night.

Garfield goes along the downstage corridor to the bathroom

Julie What's good about it.

Julie gets into the lift and goes down

Mrs Garfield Right, now they've gone this room's vacant. I shall move in here with my husband.
Manager Oh very well, madam, if you insist.
Mrs Garfield I do. Kindly tell that insolent porter to move my harp back in here immediately.
Manager Yes, madam. I don't know what he'll say, but I've got a pretty good idea.

Mrs Garfield I'm going to get my things and go to bed.

She goes out, followed by the Manager and Michele, and opens the door to Room 18

George, we're moving. Oh! Now where's he gone? (*To the Manager*) Kindly find my husband and inform him that we've moved.

Manager (*wearily*) Yes, madam. Do you know where Mr Garfield is?

Mrs Garfield Dr Garfield. And if I knew where he was I'd go and find him myself.

Mrs Garfield goes into Room 18

Michele I suppose I shall have to go into Eighteen on my own now.

Manager No, no, you should be in Twelve, with your husband.

Michele My husband?

Manager Yes, Mr Smith.

Michele Oh him. I'd forgotten about him.

Manager Forgotten about him?

Michele I mean I'd forgotten about him changing the room. I don't know where it is.

Manager Follow me, madam. I'll have the porter move your things.

The Manager shows Michele into Room 12. Garfield comes from the bathroom and goes to Room 18. He just gets the door ajar when the Manager returns

Ah, Mr Smith.

Garfield quickly shuts the door

Garfield Ah!!

Manager Have you seen Dr Garfield?

Garfield No. I mean, what do you want him for?

Manager I want to tell him that he and his wife are in Twelve A now.

Garfield Oh, don't worry. I'll tell him. I know where he is.

Manager Oh, thank you, sir. I've put your wife in Twelve.

Garfield I thought you said Twelve A.

Manager No, no, that's Mrs Garfield.

Garfield That's what I said.

Manager No, I'm talking about your wife, sir, Mrs Smith.

Garfield Mrs Smith? Oh, yes I remember, that Mrs Smith. I mean I remember that—Mrs Smith wanted to move.

Manager Oh I see, sir. May I wish you a happy honeymoon night.

Garfield What? Oh yes. Good night. (*He goes to open the door of Room 12a*)

Manager Oh no, sir, that's not your room.

Garfield What? Oh yes of course. How silly of me. (*He goes to Room 12*)

Manager Good night, sir.

Garfield goes into Room 12

Michele (*off*) Get out, you brute!

Garfield (*off*) Ow!!

Garfield comes out like a rocket, clutching his stomach

Bit shy. First-night nerves. I think I'll just pop to the bathroom.

Garfield hurries off to the bathroom downstage. Albert enters along the upstage corridor

Albert You'll have to come down and sort it out. I can't cope on my own.
Manager What's the matter now?
Albert It's them lovebirds. She's in the 'all crying her eyes out and he's locked out on the doorstep shouting his head off, trying to get in. It's like a ruddy madhouse down there.
Manager Oh good gracious. We could lose a star over this.
Albert Yes, then we wouldn't have any, would we.
Manager This is terrible. Move the luggage in Twelve A to Twelve, the luggage in Eighteen to Twelve A and you've put the harp in the wrong room. You know it should be in Twelve A.
Albert (*muttering*) Go to 'ell!
Manager What did you say?
Albert I know it well!

Albert knocks and enters Room 18. The Manager reacts and goes off along the upstage corridor

(*Off*) I've come for your bloody instrument of torture again.
Mrs Garfield (*off*) Don't be so rude. And mind you don't drop it.

Albert comes out struggling with golf clubs, cases and harp, muttering darkly

Music, off. In Room 14, Douglas starts playing the theme from Beethoven's Ninth Symphony on his French horn, fortissimo. Albert, startled, drops the harp on his foot. He hops about in agony

Albert Ow!! Me flaming foot! I knew I was allergic to harps! (*Shouting*) Shut up! Shut your row! There's people here trying to get some kip.

The music stops, but Douglas plays on. Albert goes to the door of Room 14 and bangs on it

Belt up, for Gawd's sake! If you don't shut up I'll stuff that bugle up your bracket.

The horn stops abruptly

That's better. (*Bellowing*) Now let's have a bit of peace and quiet! (*He goes towards the harp*)

Douglas comes out of Room 14, carrying his French horn

Douglas Stop making that noise, I can't hear myself playing.

Douglas goes back into Room 14

Albert You're bloody lucky. Everyone else can.

Albert mutters even more darkly, and lifts the harp. Douglas starts to play again, Albert takes the harp into Room 12a and plonks it and the luggage down

Mrs Garfield comes out of Room 18 carrying her clothes, and goes into Room 12a

Bloomin' 'orrible row.

Mrs Garfield Yes, you're quite right. His embrasure's too slack.

Albert Is it? If he's not careful I'll tighten it for him. (*He gets Michele's luggage*)

Mrs Garfield Take that food away. It attracts mice.

Albert Not in this hotel it won't.

Mrs Garfield You don't mean there aren't any mice here?

Albert No I mean they won't eat our food.

Mrs Garfield goes into the bathroom

Albert wheels the trolley out, with the luggage

Evelyn comes out of Room 14, meeting Albert in the corridor

Evelyn Oh I can't stand it. Just a minute, Porter.

Albert Oh my Gawd, another one. What do you want?

Evelyn I'm looking for a lemon. Ah, can I have one of those?

Albert Help yourself.

Evelyn Thank you. (*She takes a piece of lemon*)

Evelyn goes back into Room 14

The lift starts to come up

Albert What's she up to? (*He opens the door to Room 12, throws the case in*) Your luggage, madam. (*He shuts the door*)

In Room 14, the horn slowly subsides with gurgles

Douglas (*off*) You stupid cow! Don't suck that, I can't blow.

Evelyn (*off*) Exactly.

Albert reacts and goes off along the upstage corridor. The lift doors open and the Manager comes out, followed by Julie. He is carrying her case. She has a handkerchief to her nose. The lift doors remain open

Manager No need to upset yourself, madam. I'll put you in Number Eighteen. It's very nice and it is a single. Please don't cry, madam.

Julie I'm not crying. It's that awful smell of cheap perfume in the lift.

Manager I shall have to tell that woman she must remove herself.

The Manager shows Julie into Room 18

Here you are, madam. You won't be disturbed again. (*He gives her the case*) Good night, madam. (*He closes the door*)

The Manager goes down in the lift. Outside Room 12a, hands appear on the balcony balustrade. Slowly Clifford's head appears, as he heaves him-

self up and over. He is dishevelled and still very unsteady. Ivy is hanging round his neck. He totters into Room 12a

Clifford Squirrel? Squirrel? No Squirrel. I'll go to bed and wait for her. (*He gets into bed, pulling the clothes over his head*)

Mrs Garfield comes out of the bathroom. She puts her make-up bag on the chair

There is a snore from the bed

Mrs Garfield George, trust you to drop off the moment you get into bed. Not even a good night.

Garfield comes on from the bathroom downstage

Mrs Garfield puts out the light and gets into bed. Garfield enters Room 12a as Clifford snores again

Garfield Oh for goodness sake, Winifred, stop snoring.
Mrs Garfield I'm not snoring, it's you.
Garfield Don't talk rubbish. I'm not even in bed.

There is another snore

Mrs Garfield What?

Another snore

Garfield It's you. You did it again.

Mrs Garfield puts the light on, and sits up in bed

Mrs Garfield Then who the devil . . . ?

Clifford sits and throws his arms round Mrs Garfield

Clifford Squirrel, you've come back to me.
Mrs Garfield Aah! Help! Get him off!
Garfield Good God. He's at it again. And with my wife. The man's got no taste at all.
Clifford I want a little nutkin. I want a little nutkin.

Mrs Garfield pushes Clifford away forcibly

Mrs Garfield Get off me, you brute! (*She gets out of bed, and grabs a golf club to defend herself*)
Clifford Come on, Squirrel. Badger wants it. Let Badger have it. (*He passes out and subsides into the bed*)
Mrs Garfield He's passed out. George, do something.
Garfield Yes I will. I'll go down and have that large whisky.
Mrs Garfield Oh, you're useless! I'm not staying in this room a moment longer alone with a drunken rapist. I shall move in with Michele.
Garfield What about me?
Mrs Garfield You're not going in there. You can go back into Eighteen, it's empty. (*She gathers up her things*) I shall phone the porter and tell

him to move my harp in with you at once. You guard it, nothing's safe with that man.

Mrs Garfield sweeps out and into Room 12, still carrying the golf club

Michele (*off*) Oh, Mrs Garfield . . .
Garfield I think I'll ring down for a whole bottle of whisky. (*He leaves Room 12a, goes to Room 18, and opens the door*)

Julie screams

I beg your pardon. (*He closes the door quickly*) Don't mind me, I am a doctor. I need that bottle. Where's the Manager?

Garfield goes off along the upstage corridor. Evelyn comes in along the balcony outside Room 12a. She sees the bottle of gin on the bedside table

Evelyn Ah there it is.

She picks up the bottle and takes a swig. There is a snore from Clifford

So sorry, wrong room

The lift starts to come up. Evelyn staggers across to the dressing-room and opens the door

Ah, this is my room.

Evelyn goes into the dressing-room, closing the door. The lift door opens and Garfield comes out, followed by the Manager

Manager Mr Smith, I've told you before. You should be in Twelve with Mrs Smith.
Garfield I can't go in there. She's sleeping with Mrs Garfield.
Manager Good gracious, and on her honeymoon, too. That really is too permissive.
Garfield Don't be stupid. They're not like that. You'll have to get that lunatic out of Twelve A. Then I can go in there.
Manager What!! Oh, this is too much. I can't bear it. I'm going to bed. My own bed. By myself and I'm staying there.

The Manager goes into the lift. The lift doors close and the lift goes down

Garfield I suppose I'll have to sit up downstairs with that bottle.

Albert enters along the upstage corridor

Porter, I want a bottle of whisky in the lounge.
Albert I want a bit of kip in my cubbyhole, but I can't get it. I'm not your servant, you know. You'll have to wait till I can open me cupboard.
Garfield Well, be sharp about it.
Albert (*muttering*) Great berk!
Garfield What did you say?
Albert I hate work!

Garfield goes off along the upstage corridor

Albert goes into Room 12a, looks at the harp with loathing

You know what you could do with don't you, a damned good plucking. I'm not moving you no more, and I'm going to tell her. What do they think this is, a ruddy hotel? (*He goes to Room 18, knocks and enters*) I'm not moving that . . . Oh, blimey!

Albert comes out quickly, Julie screams, off. Clifford sits up in bed quickly

Clifford Squirrel!
Julie (*off*) Badger! Help!

Douglas starts tooting on the French horn, off. Julie screams

Albert Blimey it's the Charge of the Light Brigade. I'm off.

Albert goes off along the upstage corridor

Clifford leaps out of bed, runs towards the door, he trips and goes headlong into the harp. His head goes in between the strings. N.B. This is a trick harp. Clifford tries to get free, but gets even more entangled

Julie comes out of Room 18. She is now in her nightdress and dressing-gown

Julie Oh! Badger's caught in a trap.
Clifford Squirrel! Squirrel! I'm stuck!
Julie Oh poor Badger, let me help you.

Clifford finally goes a cartwheel with the harp and ends up sitting on the bed with the harp between his knees, the right way up, and he twangs it

Clifford I think I've tamed it now.
Julie Oh my poor Badger. Where does it hurt? I'll kiss it better.
Clifford (*pleased*) Oh—no, perhaps you'd better not, it might start your hiccups again.
Julie Oh Badger, you're so brave. You tried to save Squirrel from that dreadful man.
Clifford I wouldn't let anyone harm you, Squirrel, not ever. They're all trying to spoil our honeymoon and I'm not going to let them.
Julie But what about those women and that man? You were in bed with them.
Clifford No, they were in bed with me. I didn't want them. They forced themselves on me.
Julie Oh Badger, I'm so glad. I don't think I could go through our married life like that.
Clifford Neither could I. I was made for you and you were made for me. After all, we saved ourselves for each other.
Julie Would you like me to get my things?
Clifford Oh yes I would. That's what I'd like most of all.
Julie I'll only be two ticks.

Julie goes into Room 18

Clifford moves the harp to the side

Clifford (*calling across to her*) We're going to have such fun when we get into our little nest together.

Julie puts her head out of Room 18

Julie Not so loud, Badger. (*Hic, hic, hic*)

Julie goes back into Room 18

Clifford (*to himself*) At least I hope we're going to have fun.
Julie (*off*) We're going to live happily ever after, aren't we, Badger.
Clifford Yes we are, Squirrel. And I promise I'll never even look at another woman again.

Evelyn staggers out of the dressing-room

Evelyn I'm going to complain to the Manager. There's no bed in my room.
Clifford Oh my God! What are you doing in there?
Julie (*off*) What did you say, Badger?
Clifford (*going to the door*) I said, what are you doing in there, Squirrel?
Julie (*off*) Don't get impatient, I shan't be a second.

Evelyn staggers towards the bed

Evelyn That's a nice bed.
Clifford (*running to her*) No! No! You mustn't.
Julie (*off*) I'm coming now, Badger.
Clifford Quick, she mustn't find you. (*He pushes Evelyn towards the dressing-room*)
Evelyn But I'm lost.
Clifford I will be if she sees you.

Clifford pushes Evelyn into the dressing-room and closes the door just as Julie enters Room 12a carrying her case and clothes

Julie What's Badger doing?
Clifford Er—I was just putting something in the dressing-room.
Julie Oh, I have got a nice tidy husband. I'd better put my things away as well. (*She goes towards the dressing-room*)
Clifford No! I mean I shouldn't do that. I've just looked inside, it's full of moths.
Julie Well why did you put something in there then?
Clifford Well, what I put in there was moth-eaten already.
Julie All right then, I'll put them on the chair for now. (*She does so. Nervously*) Er—shall we settle down for the night, then?
Clifford No, we can't. I mean, Squirrel hasn't cleaned her little toothy-pegs yet.
Julie No, so I haven't.
Clifford Naughty Squirrel. Take a nice long time.
Julie Oh, I shan't be a minute.
Clifford Oh, but you must . . . I mean, you must do them thoroughly. I'll just have a little walk on the balcony, while you're doing it.
Julie How thoughtful you are, Badger. (*Taking her sponge-bag*) You think of everything.

Julie goes into the bathroom and shuts the door

Water runs in the bathroom

Clifford opens the dressing-room door and drags Evelyn out

Clifford Come on, quick. I've got to get you out of here.
Evelyn (*holding up the bottle of gin*) He was a lovely soldier. I was with him when he died. Wheee!

She throws the bottle up in the air. Clifford just manages to catch it. He puts it on the bedside table. She has now eluded him and totters to the bed

I must have reinforcements. (*She bends down and gets the bottle of champagne, which she hid under the bed. She holds it up and salutes it*) Brigadier Bubbly. Up boys and at 'em.
Clifford Please. You must get out of here.

Evelyn staggers back to the dressing-room

Evelyn Certainly. If you knows of a better 'ole, go to it!

Clifford dashes to her and tries to take her to the room door, but she is hard to shift

Clifford Not in there again please. Out there.
Evelyn Kiss me good night, Sergeant Major. (*She envelops him in a bear hug*)

The water in the bathroom stops running

Julie (*off*) All finished, Badger!
Clifford Oh no!
Evelyn (*singing*) Tuck me in my little wooden bed.

Evelyn still has him in a vice-like hug and starts to dance, so that as they gather momentum they gyrate into the dressing-room. The door closes, just as Julie comes out of the bathroom

Julie (*calling out to the balcony*) You can go in now Badger. I've put some paste on your little brushikins. (*She takes off her dressing-gown, jumps into bed and pulls up the bedclothes to her neck, almost in one movement. She switches out the light and hiccups several times*)

Clifford comes out of the dressing-room

Clifford Are you asleep, Squirrel?
Julie Yes. (*She has violent hiccups, which make her bounce in the bed*)

Clifford dashes into the bathroom and turns on the tap

Clifford (*off*) I'm doing my toothy-pegs, Squirrel.

Clifford tiptoes rapidly back to the dressing-room and half carries Evelyn out

Immediately Douglas's voice is heard from the balcony

Douglas (*off*) Evelyn! Evelyn! Where are you?
Clifford Oh my God, it's your husband! He'll have me orchestrated.

Clifford quickly goes back with Evelyn into the dressing-room and shuts the door. Douglas appears in the french windows, looks in and sees the gin bottle: he picks it up and puts on the light

Douglas Come on, let's be having you.

He pulls the bedclothes right back to reveal a terrified hiccuping Julie. She has one hand over her eyes

Julie Oh Badger, I can't look. (*More violent hiccuping*)
Douglas I'm so sorry, I'm looking for a woman.

Julie takes her hand from her eyes and sees Douglas. She screams and sits up, pulls the bedclothes right up to her chin and hiccups like an earthquake

Clifford comes bounding out of the dressing-room, shutting the door behind him

Clifford What's going on? (*He runs to Julie*) Julie, are you all right? You're hiccuping. I've never seen them this bad. (*He rounds on Douglas*) What have you been doing to my wife?!
Julie He came out of the night and pulled everything off me. (*More and more hiccups*)
Clifford What! How dare you attack my wife.
Douglas I didn't. It was a mistake. I thought she was my wife.
Clifford Your wife in here? I've never heard such a ridiculous idea!
Douglas No. You see she wanders about when she's had a few—when she's had a few hours' sleep. She wanders about in her sleep.
Clifford Well, she's not here, so you'd better look somewhere else right away.
Douglas Yes I will. Sorry to have troubled you. (*He starts to go*)

There is a pop and chink from the dressing-room. Douglas turns back

What was that?
Clifford I didn't hear anything.
Julie I did. It came from the dressing-room.

There is another chink

There it is again.
Clifford I didn't hear it again.
Douglas Wait a minute. I'd know that sound anywhere. Let me have a look.

He advances towards the dressing-room. Clifford tries to bar his way

Clifford No, no, it's the moths, they're having a party.
Douglas I know what party's in there. And I know the only way to get her out. Cheers! Bottoms up!

Evelyn staggers out holding the champagne bottle. She tips it upside down to show it's empty

Gotcher!

Evelyn I'll have a gin. (*She subsides into the armchair*)

Julie Clifford, what were you doing with that woman in that room? (*She hiccups*)

Douglas rounds on Clifford

Douglas Yes. Wait a minute. What were you doing with her in there?

Clifford She bent down and took it out and made me go in.

Douglas What!

Douglas grabs Clifford

Clifford She wanted me to tuck her up in bed.

Douglas What?!

Douglas throws Clifford on to the bed. Julie is having raging hiccups

Julie Get off, you filthy beast!

Douglas How dare you get my wife in that condition, and then take advantage of her.

Clifford No, no, you don't understand. I only did it so as not to upset my wife.

Julie Go away. I never want to see you again.

Douglas (*advancing menacingly towards Clifford*) Don't worry. By the time I've finished with him, there won't be anything left to see.

Clifford (*backing*) No, no, I'm innocent.

Douglas I'll teach you to meddle with my wife.

Evelyn D'you know, he made me go in there to pop my cork.

Douglas What?! I'll kill you for this. (*He lunges at Clifford*)

Clifford (*dodging*) No, no.

Clifford runs off along the balcony away from the corridor

Douglas Come back, you swine!

Douglas runs out after Clifford

The lift starts to come up

Evelyn I must go and bury this soldier. (*She drops it over the balcony*)

There is a cry from Albert, off

Albert (*off*) Watch where you're chucking your empties.

Julie I can't stand it any more. I've had all I can take. (*She gets out of bed and puts on her dressing-gown*)

Evelyn Well I haven't, but I've forgotten where I put it, very frustrating. Ah, I've just seen the light. (*She gets up on the bed and retrieves the gin from the hanging bowl-light*) I'm just going to clean my teeth.

Evelyn goes into the bathroom. Albert comes out of the lift

Julie Mother was right. All men are the same. I never want to see another one.

Albert, entering Room 12a, comes face to face with Julie, who screams

Albert What's all this row going on?
Julie Keep away! Keep away!
Albert Shut up and get into bed!
Julie No! No! Don't touch me, you disgusting old man! (*She runs out to the corridor*)
Albert Who are you calling disgusting? You watch your bloody language!

Julie runs into Room 18 and shuts the door

Music starts, off, and occurs from time to time during the chase

They'd better see me right. My ears is allergic to noise.

Clifford, hotly pursued by Douglas, runs along the balcony from one side to the other

Douglas Come here! Come here!
Clifford No, no!

Douglas and Clifford run off

Albert Oi! What's going on? You can't run races along the balcony. It's against the rules.

Albert runs off after Douglas and Clifford. Garfield enters along the upstage corridor, holding a half-full bottle of whisky

Garfield I'm not staying down there. I'm going to sleep in my own bed. Which is it?

He looks around baffled, then opens the door to Room 18. Julie screams, he quickly shuts the door

What's she got against doctors?

The lift descends

Screams come from Michele and Mrs Garfield in Room 12

Michele runs out and off along the downstage corridor. Clifford follows and goes off into Room 14

Michele Help, help, we're being attacked.
Clifford Don't let him get me, I'm on my honeymoon.

Mrs Garfield comes out of Room 12

Mrs Garfield Somebody get the Manager. (*She sees Garfield*) George defend me, he's after my body.
Garfield Poor fellow, doesn't know what he's doing.
Mrs Garfield Neither do you. You're drunk. Leaving me alone to be attacked by a lunatic. He'll be after my harp next.
Garfield What's he going to do with it, pluck it or . . .
Mrs Garfield (*quickly*) He's not doing anything with it. I'm going to put on my dressing-gown and guard it. He won't touch anything of mine.

Mrs Garfield goes into Room 12

Garfield Not if he's got any sense he won't.

Douglas and Albert run on in the upstage corridor. At the same time Michele runs on in the downstage corridor

Douglas (*off*) Where are you? (*As he enters*) You're going to get it whether you like it or not.

Douglas and Michele meet downstage. Michele turns and runs off downstage, followed by Douglas

Albert (*following them*) You can't do it in the corridor, it's not allowed.

Albert runs off after them

Garfield Stop! You can't do that to her, I saw her first!

Garfield runs off after Albert. Clifford comes out of Room 14 and runs into Room 12a. He goes to the balcony

Douglas (*off, on the balcony*) You can't get away from me!

Clifford turns and runs into the bathroom. Douglas runs on from the balcony

I'll teach you to molest my wife!

The lift comes up

Douglas runs across the balcony and off. Clifford hastily backs out of the bathroom

Clifford Sorry, madam. I didn't know you were sitting there having a drink. (*He shuts the door and goes up to the balcony*)

Albert (*off* UR) Come back 'ere all of you!

Clifford runs to the door of Room 12a

Albert runs across the balcony after Douglas. At the same time the Manager comes out of the lift, leaving the doors open. Clifford runs past him into the lift and closes the doors. After a second he opens them and staggers out, choking

Clifford I've been gassed!

Clifford runs out along the downstage corridor. At the same time Albert runs on along the upstage corridor

Manager Albert! What is going on?

Albert They've all gone mad. This place has sent them all allergic.

Manager What are you talking about?

Albert They're all running round in their nightclothes like a lot of frustrated sex maniacs, trying to have a go at each other.

Manager Good heavens, it's an orgy! You must stop them, Albert. Our name will stink after this.

Albert Yes, just like your flaming perfume.
Manager My perfume. There's nothing the matter with my perfume. I can't smell anything.
Albert Then there must be something wrong with your nose.

Mrs Garfield comes out from Room 12, brandishing the golf club

Manager Don't be so impertinent. You're sacked!
Albert (*muttering*) Stupid fart!
Manager What did you say?
Albert I said stupid fart!
Mrs Garfield I'm going into Twelve A and I'm going to stay there for the night.
Manager Stupid fart!
Mrs Garfield What?! How dare you! I shall see that you're sacked. (*She goes into Room 12a and shuts the door*)
Albert (*chuckling*) See you down the Labour.

Albert goes out along the upstage corridor

The Manager closes the lift gate and doors. In Room 12a, Mrs Garfield moves her harp next to the bed and gets in. She lays the golf club down ready to hand, puts the light out and lies down

Douglas (*off*) I can see you! It's no good running away!
Manager Oh, they're at it again! Stop it at once!

The Manager runs out along the upstage corridor. Clifford dashes into Room 12a from the balcony and dives under the bed. Douglas runs after him, and leaps on top of Mrs Garfield

Douglas Gotcher! I'm going to give it to you now.
Mrs Garfield No! No! Get off!

Albert runs in from the balcony

Albert Out of 'ere, you! (*He launches himself at Douglas*)

The three of them tussle on the bed

The Manager comes in from the balcony and switches on the light

Manager Stop, stop I say, stop!

He tries to separate them, Mrs Garfield takes the rules in a frame from behind the door, goes to hit Douglas with them, and crowns the Manager instead. The Manager staggers about

Oh, you've broken the rules.

The Manager goes off by the upstage corridor

Mrs Garfield (*to Douglas*) Get out, you monster!
Douglas I thought you were a man.
Mrs Garfield How dare you!
Douglas I was damn nearly right.

Mrs Garfield bundles Douglas out of the door

Mrs Garfield Get out before I call the police.

Evelyn staggers out of the bathroom and slips into bed unseen by them

Mrs Garfield shuts the door of Room 12a and gets into bed

Douglas goes out by the upstage corridor

Garfield (*off*) Michele! Michele!
Michele (*off*) Keep your hands off me!

Michele runs on through the french windows into Room 12a and dives under the bed

Clifford comes out from under the bed and gets tangled up in the harp

Garfield runs on through the french windows

Garfield Michele! Come here, you gorgeous creature.

He grabs Mrs Garfield, who sits up in bed

Mrs Garfield George, what do you think you're doing? I thought you were the organist.
Garfield What! I thought you were Michele.
Mrs Garfield What?!
Garfield I mean . . .
Michele (*coming out from under the bed*) Keep him away from me, he isn't normal.

Douglas comes on through the french windows

Evelyn sits up in bed and grabs the whisky bottle from Garfield

Evelyn Gotcher!
Douglas My God! He's got three women and a man now. Let me get at him! (*He runs round below the bed*)
Clifford No! No!

Clifford runs over the bed and out of the french windows on the downstage corridor side. Douglas pursues him

Mrs Garfield Get off me! How dare you!
Evelyn Mind my bottle!

Mrs Garfield gets out of bed

Mrs Garfield George, I demand an explanation.
Garfield I'm trying to think of one.
Michele Try the truth for a change, you sex-mad homosexual!
Mrs Garfield What?! I'll have you struck off. Better than that I'll strike you off myself. (*She grabs a golf club*)
Garfield (*backing*) No, no, that's my favourite putter.

Garfield runs off through the french windows on the downstage corridor side

Mrs Garfield I'll sink you and I don't care how many strokes I take!

Mrs Garfield runs off after Garfield

Michele (*grabbing a wood from the golf bag*) Wait a minute, Mrs Garfield, don't sink him till I've hit him in the bunker.

Michele runs off after the Garfields

Evelyn This is a very noisy Golf Club. I shall complain to the Steward. (*She takes a swig of whisky*)

Douglas (*off, in Room 14*) I'll crown you, you swine!

There is a loud crash off in Room 14, and a yelp from Clifford

Clifford staggers out of Room 14, with the French horn jammed on his head

Clifford Julie, Julie, help me! I've got the horn!

Clifford runs into Room 12a, trying to get the horn off; he staggers on to the balcony, and off

Evelyn Oh my goodness, a gladiator. I usually only see little green men. (*She hides under the bedclothes*)

Douglas runs out of Room 14, and across downstage to Room 12a

Douglas (*entering Room 12a*) Where are you? I haven't finished with you yet. (*He looks in, sees no-one there and goes to the door of Room 18*) Must have gone in here. Right, I'll have you this time.

Douglas goes into Room 18. Julie screams off, and dashes out and into Room 12a, shutting the door behind her

Julie Clifford, Clifford, don't let him have me!

Clifford comes on from the balcony carrying the horn

Clifford (*opening the dressing-room door*) Quick, Squirrel, in here.

Julie runs straight into the dressing-room, Clifford follows and shuts the door just as Douglas, who has come out of Room 18, opens the door to Room 12a

Douglas You won't get away from me. (*He picks up empty gin bottle as he goes*) I'm going to break this over your head.

Douglas goes out to the balcony and off on the downstage corridor side

Evelyn (*getting out of bed hastily*) No, Douglas don't do that. There may be a drop left in it.

Evelyn staggers off after Douglas. The Manager runs on from the upstage corridor with the framed rules still round his neck

Manager No, Albert, don't touch me with that thing! (*He goes to the lift and opens the doors*)

Albert comes on along the upstairs corridor with a large saw in his hand

Albert Come here, I'll have it off in a jiffy, and your head as well.

The Manager shoots into the lift, leaving the doors open. Albert holds his nose and follows. The Manager runs out just as Garfield, Mrs Garfield, Michele, Douglas and Evelyn run on from the downstage corridor across the stage, all shouting. They sweep the Manager back into the lift, and all follow in

The doors close and the lift starts to go up and down erratically between floors, to the accompaniment of shouts and screams. The lift comes to a stop between floors

(*Off, in the lift*) My God, now you've done it. It's stuck!

Cries of "let us out" and "help", etc.

We'll all be gassed! By Chanel Number Five.

Clifford and Julie come out of the dressing-room in Room 12a, hand in hand

They have heard the shouts: they come out of Room 12a and go to the lift. They see the indicator is stuck

Julie Whatever's happened?
Clifford They've all got stuck in the lift between floors.
Julie Oh how awful, we'd better try and get them out.
Clifford Yes. Wait a minute, no. Let them stay there. They've caused us quite enough frustration for one night. Now it's their turn.
Julie Oh Badger, you are a devil.
Clifford I know.

They giggle

(*Calling to the lift*) See you all in the morning. Nightie-night.
Julie Sleep tight.
Clifford / **Julie** } Let's all hope that the bugs don't bite. } (*Speaking together*)

They trip into 12a and shut the door

Clifford Safe at last in woodland.
Julie Yes, our own little fairy dell.
Clifford Oh Squirrel.
Julie Oh Badger. Let's go to bed.
Clifford Do you really really want to?
Julie Really really. And I don't feel a little bit sleepy.
Clifford (*almost speechless*) Oh Squirrel. (*He suddenly realizes*) You—you haven't got the hiccups.
Julie No, I haven't. Isn't it marvellous. Let's go to bed and do it now.
Clifford It?
Julie Yes, you know, what we've saved ourselves for—"it", darling.
Clifford Oh, that "it", darling. (*Suddenly he breaks out into uncontrolled monumental hiccups: distressed*) Oh—(*hic*)—Squi—(*hic*)—rrel—(*hic, hic, hic*)

Julie (*bursting into tears*) Oh Badger . . .

We hear renewed shouting from the lift and music, off, less the harp and French horn, as—

the CURTAIN *falls*

FURNITURE AND PROPERTY LIST

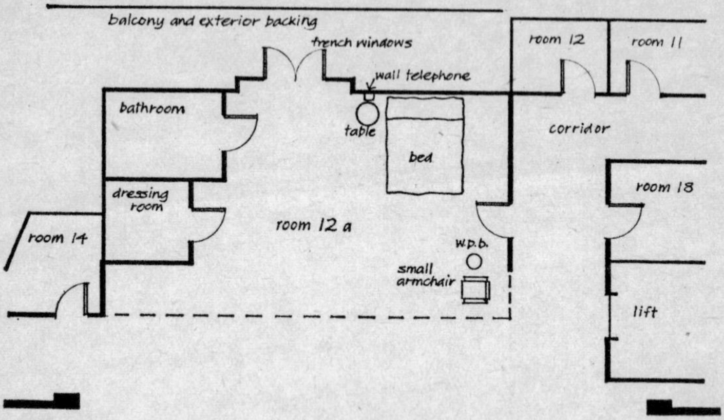

ACT I

On stage: ROOM 12a:
Double bed and bedding, with trick spring. *Beside it:* bag of tools
Bed table. *On it:* carafe of water, glass
Small armchair. *Beside it:* wastepaper-basket
Dressing-table
Stool
Linked light switches above bed and by main door
On wall above dressing-room: mirror
On wall above bed table: house telephone
Behind door: framed set of rules
Carpet
Window curtains

CORRIDOR:
Indicator above lift
Strip of shabby red carpet
Upstage end: Notice reading "STAIRS AND FIRE EXIT"
Downstage end: Notice reading: "TO BATHROOM AND W.C."

Off stage: Perfume spray **(Manager)**
Tray with pint of bitter and Babycham **(Albert)**
Cello **(Albert)**
Piccolo case **(Albert)**
Bottle of after-shave **(Manager)**
Aerosol spray (in bathroom) **(Manager)**

Cologne stick, foot spray **(Manager)**
Golf ball, putter, golf bag **(Garfield)**
Suitcases with clothing and nightwear **(Michele)**
Piece of broken washbasin **(Manager)**
4 bed legs **(Albert)**
Harp **(Albert)**
Mrs Garfield's suitcases with clothing and nightwear **(Albert)**
Clifford's and **Julie**'s suitcases with clothing and nightwear **(Albert)**
Michele's make-up case **(Garfield)**
Knitting-bag and wool **(Mrs Garfield)**
Key **(Mrs Garfield)**
Music case with music, trick stand **(Albert)**
Trolley with champagne, sandwiches decorated with lettuce and lemon wedges **(Albert)**
French horn in case, suitcase with clothing and nightwear **(Douglas)**
Holdall full of rattling gin bottles **(Evelyn)**
Tray with glass of sherry **(Albert)**
Towel (in bathroom) **(Julie)**
Aerosol can **(Albert)**

Personal: **Garfield**: string-backed gloves, ring
Mrs Garfield: handbag with coins, tablets
Clifford: coins
Evelyn: handbag
Julie: handbag
Albert: grubby handkerchief

ACT II

Off stage: Towel, sponge-bag **(Douglas)**
Serviette with mushed salad **(Garfield)**
Glass of sherry on tray **(Manager)**
Tray with glass of malted milk, plate of cream crackers **(Albert)**
Sponge-bag **(Garfield)**
Luggage trolley **(Albert)**
Ivy **(Clifford)**
Trick harp **(Albert)**
Half-full bottle of whisky **(Garfield)**
Hacksaw **(Albert)**

Personal: **Julie**: Handkerchief

LIGHTING PLOT

Property fittings required: pendant, hanging bowl lamp above bed
Interior: A bedroom and corridor. The same scene throughout

ACT I Evening

To open: All artificial lighting on

No cues

ACT II Evening

To open: As Act I

Cue 1 **Michele** switches out lights (Page 52)
Black-out in Room 12a

Cue 2 **Julie** switches on lights (Page 53)
Full up in Room 12a

Cue 3 **Mrs Garfield** switches out lights (Page 62)
Black-out in Room 12a

Cue 4 **Mrs Garfield** switches on lights (Page 62)
Full up in Room 12a

Cue 5 **Julie** switches out lights (Page 66)
Black-out in Room 12a

Cue 6 **Clifford** switches on lights (Page 67)
Full up in Room 12a

Cue 7 **Mrs Garfield** switches out lights (Page 71)
Black-out in Room 12a

Cue 8 **Manager** switches on lights (Page 71)
Full up in Room 12a

EFFECTS PLOT

NOTE: Unless a definite "music off" cue is given, the length of time of the music cues is at the discretion of the director

ACT I

Cue 1	As CURTAIN rises *Sound of discordant musical instruments tuning up*	(Page 1)
Cue 2	**Manager**: ". . . piccolo, aren't you?" *Double bassoon note*	(Page 1)
Cue 3	**Manager**: "The drinks at last." *Sound of lift ascending*	(Page 1)
Cue 4	**Manager**: "Oh, really." *Sound of lift descending*	(Page 3)
Cue 5	**Manager** sprays pillow *Instruments tuning up*	(Page 3)
Cue 6	**Albert**: ". . . at the same time." *Lift ascends*	(Page 4)
Cue 7	**Garfield**: ". . . playing golf in Cromer." *Telephone rings*	(Page 6)
Cue 8	**Garfield**: "Come on." *Lift descends*	(Page 7)
Cue 9	**Albert**: "Soon done that." *China crash*	(Page 7)
Cue 10	**Manager**: ". . . bed leg in Fourteen." *Lift ascends*	(Page 7)
Cue 11	**Mrs Garfield**: ". . . efforts to the contrary." *Lift descends*	(Page 10)
Cue 12	**Mrs Garfield** enters Room 18 *Lift ascends*	(Page 10)
Cue 13	**Michele**: ". . . weeny bit squiffy." *Lift descends*	(Page 10)
Cue 14	**Garfield**: "Sssh!" *Lift ascends*	(Page 10)
Cue 15	**Garfield** enters lift *Lift descends*	(Page 11)
Cue 16	**Julie**: ". . . come into us." *Music*	(Page 11)

Cue 17	**Michele** exits on balcony *Lift ascends*	(Page 14)
Cue 18	**Clifford** enters lift *Lift descends*	(Page 14)
Cue 19	**Garfield** pushes lift button *Lift ascends*	(Page 19)
Cue 20	**Garfield** enters lift *Lift descends*	(Page 19)
Cue 21	**Michele**: ". . . giving us the best room." *Lift ascends*	(Page 20)
Cue 22	**Mrs Garfield** enters lift *Lift descends*	(Page 21)
Cue 23	**Julie** presses button *Lift ascends*	(Page 21)
Cue 24	**Julie** enters lift *Lift descends*	(Page 21)
Cue 25	**Albert**: ". . . allergic to stairs." *Lift ascends*	(Page 22)
Cue 26	**Albert** enters lift *Lift descends*	(Page 23)
Cue 27	**Mrs Garfield** presses button *Lift ascends*	(Page 23)
Cue 28	**Mrs Garfield** enters lift *Lift descends*	(Page 24)
Cue 29	**Garfield**: ". . . before she gets here?" *Lift ascends*	(Page 24)
Cue 30	**Garfield**: ". . . in your present condition." *Lift descends*	(Page 28)
Cue 31	**Mrs Garfield**: "Gotcher." *Lift ascends*	(Page 28)
Cue 32	**Garfield**: ". . . lift catches up with us." *Lift descends*	(Page 28)
Cue 33	**Garfield**: "Well, of course it is." *Lift ascends*	(Page 28)
Cue 34	**Mrs Garfield** enters lift *Lift descends*	(Page 30)
Cue 35	**Michele**: "Oh, this is too much." *Lift ascends*	(Page 31)
Cue 36	**Albert** enters lift *Lift ascends*	(Page 31)
Cue 37	**Julie**: ". . . to call a doctor." *Lift ascends*	(Page 32)
Cue 38	**Julie** bangs lift doors shut *Lift descends*	(Page 33)

Cue 39	**Douglas** blows loud notes on horn *Lift ascends*	(Page 35)
Cue 40	**Clifford:** "Badger's getting—sleepy!" *Lift descends*	(Page 37)
Cue 41	**Clifford** undresses *Lift ascends*	(Page 37)
Cue 42	**Manager** enters lift *Lift descends*	(Page 38)
Cue 43	**Clifford:** ". . taking my trousers off." *Lift ascends*	(Page 38)
Cue 44	**Dr** and **Mrs Garfield** enter lift *Lift descends*	(Page 40)
Cue 45	**Clifford** slides into bed *Lift ascends*	(Page 41)
Cue 46	As CURTAIN falls *Discordant music*	(Page 41)

ACT II

Cue 47	As CURTAIN rises *Discordant music*	(Page 42)
Cue 48	**Garfield** and **Albert** enter lift *Lift descends*	(Page 42)
Cue 49	**Michelle** goes to bathroom *Lift ascends*	(Page 43)
Cue 50	**Douglas** and **Garfield** circle *Music*	(Page 44)
Cue 51	**Mrs Garfield** enters lift *Lift descends*	(Page 44)
Cue 52	**Manager:** ". . . frustrating for your wife." *Lift ascends*	(Page 45)
Cue 53	**Julie** enters lift *Lift descends*	(Page 45)
Cue 54	**Manager:** ". . . doing in there?" *Music*	(Page 47)
Cue 55	**Mrs Garfield:** ". . . in my drawers." *Music stops*	(Page 47)
Cue 56	**Manager:** ". . . in the wrong room." *A "raspberry" is blown, echoed on various musical instruments*	(Page 47)
Cue 57	**Douglas:** ". . . rooms mixed up." *Lift ascends. Music*	(Page 48)
Cue 58	**Garfield** enters lift *Lift descends*	(Page 49)

Cue 59 **Mrs Garfield**: ". . . come near you tonight." (Page 52)
Music

Cue 60 **Manager** knocks on Room 14 (Page 52)
Lift ascends

Cue 61 **Julie** enters lift (Page 53)
Lift descends

Cue 62 **Clifford** puts glass down (Page 54)
Lift ascends

Cue 63 **Albert** enters with malted milk (Page 54)
Music. Lift descends

Cue 64 **Albert** enters Room 12a (Page 57)
Lift ascends

Cue 65 **Albert**: ". . . . must be my allergy." (Page 57)
Music

Cue 66 **Julie** enters lift (Page 58)
Lift descends

Cue 67 **Albert**: ". . . to get some kip." (Page 60)
Music stops

Cue 68 **Evelyn**: "Thank you." (Page 61)
Lift ascends

Cue 69 **Mrs Garfield**: "Not even a good night." (Page 62)
Lift descends

Cue 70 **Evelyn**: "So sorry, wrong room." (Page 63)
Lift ascends

Cue 71 **Manager** enters lift (Page 63)
Lift descends

Cue 72 **Julie** enters bathroom (Page 66)
Sound of running water

Cue 73 **Evelyn**: ". . . good night, Sergeant Major." (Page 66)
Running water stops

Cue 74 **Douglas**: "Come back, you swine!" (Page 68)
Lift ascends

Cue 75 **Albert**: ". . . your bloody language!" (Page 69)
Music—continue on and off through chase

Cue 76 **Garfield**: ". . . got against doctors?" (Page 69)
Lift descends

Cue 77 **Douglas**: ". . . *to molest my wife!*" (Page 70)
Lift ascends

Cue 78 **Douglas**: ". . . crown you, you swine." (Page 73)
Loud crash from Room 14

Cue 79 General exit into lift (Page 74)
Lift goes up and down erratically, then sticks

Cue 80 **Julie**: "Oh, Badger . . ." (Page 75)
Music until CURTAIN *falls*

MADE AND PRINTED IN GREAT BRITAIN BY
LATIMER TREND & COMPANY LTD PLYMOUTH
MADE IN ENGLAND